PRAISE FOR
WRITE AND PUBLISH ORGANICALLY

"From small seeds, great plants grow. Sometimes these seeds grow into books. *Write and Publish Organically* is a primer, but more than that, a poem dedicated to faith-based publishing. Cathy Lawton covers the process of writing a book from germination to harvest and delivery. This book guides the aspiring author and well-published authors like me to do our best work and produce our most abundant harvest. An inspirational text for authors at every stage of their writing journey."

–Bruce Epperly

author of *Homegrown Mystics: Restoring Our Nation with the Wisdom of America's Visionaries* and many other books

"Author and publisher Cathy Lawton gives the reader a glimpse into both the soul and logistics of a Christian publisher. She eloquently shares the rich and varied sources that have influenced her work as a publisher—personally, spiritually, professionally, and logistically. The author's weaving of both the reflective and practical provides the reader—whether a publisher or author—with valuable insights and practical tips for writing, publishing, and marketing but with a sense of having enjoyed a rich conversation over a cup of coffee."

–Janyne McConnaughey, PhD

author of award-winning *Trauma in the Pews* and *Brave*

"I can't fully express my delight and joy in reading this new book, authored by Catherine Lawton. Its pages are rich with detail and word pictures that inspire good writing. The author brings a lifetime of family history that helps to cast new perspectives on building our 'gardens of words and stories.' I especially appreciate the way she, as an experienced and capable gardener, captures the adventure of writing. This book would be very appropriate for any writer or publisher, as there are many take-aways that one can easily incorporate into a writing life. I also believe it would be beneficial to anyone who likes to read a good book, because that's exactly what this is: a good book!"

–Susan Elaine Jenkins
author of *Scandalon: Running from Shame and Finding God's Scandalous Love*

"*Write and Publish Organically* is one of the most unusual writing books you will read and one that you won't soon forget. The author uses her many years of experience as a writer and publisher, as well as her biblical and theological studies. She also draws insights from her love of gardening and applies them to the various writing stages. I appreciate her encouragement to bring an integrated, authentic life to writing and marketing, and I am thankful to have a book that spurs new writing approaches."

–Judith Galblum Pex
author of *Walk the Land: A Journey on Foot through Israel* and *A People Tall & Smooth: Escape from Sudan to Israel*

"From the pen of prolific writer, poet and publisher, Catherine Lawton's latest book breaks new ground. She challenges writers to dig deep; to unearth dormant seeds within, so fresh, fearless fruit can form ... fruit that facilitates the blossoming of hope, that encourages resistance to sameness and safe ground, and provokes inclusion and connectedness. Such a harvest promises life-giving nourishment to readers hungry for healthy organic soul food."

–Alice Scott-Ferguson
poet, author of *Daughter of the Isles: A Memoir* and
Pausing in the Passing Places: Poems

"*Write and Publish Organically* is refreshingly counter-culture to much of the writing advice expressed on internet videos to write what sells, produce low-content books by the shelf full, and generate significant income with minimal effort. Cathy Lawton suggests implementing a process that's organic in nature. Three appendices that focus on publishing models, the publishing process, and marketing provide helpful reminders to those familiar with the writing/publishing process and a good primer for those new to the world of producing books. Worthy of a slow and reflective read!"

–David J. Claassen
retired pastor, author of *Kathryn's Fountain: A Novel* and
Growing Old Gracefully

"This is the most unique book I have ever read. An easy read, yet loaded with important information about writing. It artfully blends the author's life experiences, Scripture, and gardening wisdom with how to write a book, article, or even memoirs. Because the author is the owner/editor of a small press, the information in this book is invaluable. Ms. Lawton covers every critical aspect of writing and being published."

–Susan Bulanda
author of award-winning *Faithful Friends* and
God's Creatures: A Biblical View of Animals

WRITE AND PUBLISH ORGANICALLY

Dig Deep, Tend the Soil, Help Newness Emerge

Catherine Lawton

CLADACH
Publishing

© 2024 by Catherine Lawton

All rights reserved

Published by
Cladach Publishing
Greeley, CO
https://cladach.com

Published in
cooperation with

Northwind Seminary Press
Winter Garden, FL
www.northwindpress.org

Cover art: istock

Unless otherwise noted, Scripture quotations are from the New Revised Standard Version of the Bible, copyright © 1989 by the Division of Christian Education of the National Council of the Churches of Christ in the U.S.A., and used by permission.

ISBN: 9781945099366

Library of Congress Control Number: 2024917724

To my Mother
Jeanne Cummings

*whose earthly life was short,
but whose encouragement lives on*

CONTENTS

Introduction 11
Chapter 1: SOAK 23
Chapter 2: SPOKE 45
Chapter 3: EVOKE 73
Chapter 4: PROVOKE 93
Chapter 5: STOKE 113
Appendix I: Publishing Models 129
Appendix II: The Publishing Process 133
Appendix III: Marketing for Introverts .. 141
Notes 147
Bibliography 153
Acknowledgments 159

INTRODUCTION

"The biblical claim [is] that man is created to till the garden, and to 'be fruitful and multiply': our purpose is not only to know reality, but to involve ourselves in cultivating and caring for it, to encounter the world, and indeed each other, in a way that bears—always in some respects unexpected—fruit."
—D.C. Schindler

"The writing process is always open-ended as it brings something novel into my life and the world."
—Bruce Epperly

"To a large extent, this world of small presses exists as a parallel universe to the world of the large corporate publishers."
—John B. Thompson

WRITE & PUBLISH ORGANICALLY

What makes a published book a success? The number of copies sold? The amount of income produced? Praise from readers?

When publishers distribute books, they are like farmers broadcasting seeds. In the Parable of the Sower found in the Gospels, Jesus tells a story of a farmer who went out to sow seeds. Like him, we send out literary "seeds" as far and wide as we can, hoping they fall on ready, prepared soil that can and will receive the message, take it to heart, and act upon it.

In wintry times, seeds lie dormant in the ground waiting, sealed. When days grow longer and warmer, the seeds awaken, germinate, and sprout into plants that produce leaves and fruit.

Same with books. You may buy a book or be given one, but the season of your life isn't right yet. The book sits on a shelf, or under a pile of other volumes, or in a list of Kindle files you plan to read—sometime. Then one day you pick up the book, or click open the file, and start reading; and you marvel that these words are exactly what you need right *now*.

My vision of faith-based writing and publishing is like growing a garden that is not only productive but beautiful and good and true, in the sense that it helps to reveal reality and it gives life to all touched by that garden: workers, pollinators, neighbors, and consumers of the fruit.

A farmer might think, "Wow, look at all this good seed I've purchased and soil I've prepared. I'll get a huge crop, take it to market, and make lots of money." But the results may be quite different. Why? Partly because the sower does not control every aspect of the process; the wind may carry the seed places unexpected. Marauders and pests may steal and destroy.

Drought and heat waves may bake the soil hard and impenetrable. Or a deluge may wash away the topsoil and take the seed with it. Current events or economic downturns may slow demand at the market. Farming—and publishing—take vision, perseverance, and faith. One needs the desire to get their hands in the dirt. In other words, love for the process.

Sowing or casting seeds or books requires a long vision. A faith-based publisher must believe that these books, which contain kernels of life-giving truth, will be carried by the wind of the Spirit. And when prepared, personal soil receives these seeds, we pray that their message will be watered by the Living Water. The resulting fruit will be minds and hearts growing and encouraged to flourish in hopeful wholeness, spiritual insights, and joyful service that will in turn transform the world.

The writer and publisher, then, must listen to—and respond to—a call, then take steps with trust in the received vision. Esther Meek, Christian philosopher, professor and author of the books *Loving to Know* and *Longing to Know* talks about trusting ourselves to something. She uses the example of gardening. She says at first, as a beginning gardener, you totally trust the authorities' expert guidance; then as you gain experience, you begin to listen to and hear the dirt itself, then the plants, etc. "Reality turns the tables and walks into our lives," says Meek. Then she warns, "Don't distrust the real. You miss out on reality that way." She speaks of trusting the vision for your art or work.[1]

How does that vision come? How can we risk recognizing and trusting it?

First let me ask: What does sustainable, faith-based publishing by a small press look like in our postmodern, emergent, technological context? As the owner of a small, faith-based press myself, during twenty plus years of steep learning curves, amid a digital revolution, I have learned much that I can share with those who are looking to start publishing, or with writers/

publishers in need of perspective and encouragement.

As one who also enjoys gardening, I see principles of sustainable publishing in the practice of organic gardening. This comparison grounds my discussion in the pages ahead. A lot of thought, prayer, study, conversation, and experience goes into this project, not to mention error and trial, failure and success. Life is an adventure, a learning experience; and it is meant to be shared. Together let's get our hands into the dirt of publishing.

This is not only mental and spiritual work. It is sensory, experiential. For instance, I received an email from a friend who casually commented that my small press, Cladach Publishing, is a "boutique publisher." That struck me as a fitting descriptor of what we hope to offer to our authors, customers, and readers. The word "boutique" brings these words to mind: unique, hand picked, entrepreneurial, personal, expressive of community, and artsy.

In my mind I picture the shops I've walked into while sightseeing and browsing in charming, coastal villages and mountain towns. These places offer something that big box stores, as predictable and cheap as they may be, can't. As you step in the welcoming entrance, all the senses are soon pleased. You breathe the aroma of potpourri made from locally grown herbs. You are enticed by complimentary samples of coffee, herbal tea, or chocolate truffles. Beautiful music plays unobtrusively in the background. Colorful, tasteful, artfully arranged merchandise draws your eye and causes you to "ooh" and "ah." You feel a sense of appreciation for the evident care that went into selecting the articles of clothing, gift items, handmade pottery, and other specialty goods. You browse the colorful rack of local author books. You assume this boutique shop is an expression of the owner's tastes, and if you find their style appealing, you have a sense that you can trust their choices of items offered. You may think, "I'm glad I could experience this place. I want to take something home with me to remember my stop in this little town." Or perhaps, "I want to buy something to take back to my friend or family member, just to share a bit of this experience with them." The shop owner, who may even live upstairs, engages you in conversation. When you complete your purchase and walk back out onto the sidewalk with a custom printed bag in tow, you have a smile on your face and a spring in your step.

Cladach is a boutique publisher in the sense that we want to offer an alternative to over-hyped, mass-produced, predictable books that cram the catalogs and warehouses of huge publishing conglomerates. We are picky about style and content, wanting it to give you a meaningful and uplifting experience outside the box. We can offer ingenious, personal, one-of-a-kind books by authors both "down home" local and fascinatingly cosmopolitan. We can try new trends without being faddish. Quality matters to us and reflects our personal convictions. We hope our books give readers and browsers an opportunity to step off the trafficky, noisy street and breathe deeply of heavenly scents; taste morsels of beauty, goodness, and truth; and find delightful, soul-lifting discoveries.

That sounds nice; but it's not easy. It takes commitment and "applying the seat of your pants to the seat of your chair" in front of your computer, among other tasks—no matter which publishing path you take.

First, a publisher must decide on their business model. And a writer must choose which publishing model they want for themselves and their book(s). The choices are growing as I write. Traditional publishing is still around but difficult to break into and most often requires authors be agented. Self publishing has become more viable and respected in recent years. One can list cooperative publishing, book packaging, hybrid publishing, and the options are multiplying. (See the appendices for explanations of publishing models and the publishing process.)

In all this we are sustained by a sense of a call to ministry. You may ask, in what ways is publishing a ministry? Most people probably think of "ministers" as pastors, priests, or deacons. In some contexts today, people see a church and its pastor that seem to be all about appearances, numbers, buildings, programs, etc., and they ask, is that truly "ministry"? If a pastor seeks God's heart for their church and community, and serves in love, that may sound more like ministry. Ministry does not mean attracting a full sanctuary of washed and coiffed people. It may mean, instead, bringing in—or going out to—the unwashed with a bowl and a towel. People oriented. Needs oriented. Love oriented. Service oriented. Community oriented. How do we, as writers and publishers, achieve that type of ministry in a sustainable way, in the world in which we live today? Here's one way of looking at that question. Long before I started Cladach, I was a freelance writer, and I wrote this poem that was published in several periodicals:

WINDOW WASHER

We need to perceive the Truth.
Yet darkly we peer through the glass.
Clean me for use
Free me to serve
Lift me to reach
That I may wash windows for You.
Wrong doctrine obscures
Gray living besmears
Raw weather, it blurs
The pane on this side.
Provide a soft cloth—not abrasive
The vision to transcend the obstructive
And courage to rub for perfection
Searching

Editing
Polishing
Till, through one clear corner,
Someone sees You.

I like the Anne Frank quote I saw in Birmingham, Alabama, engraved on a monument erected in the context of the Civil Rights struggles of that city. It reads:

> How wonderful it is that nobody need wait a single moment before starting to improve the world.

Surely we also can be looking for ways to "improve the world" that God created, gave life to, is ever present to, and is restoring and re-creating? "For God so loved the world that he gave his only begotten son" (John 3:16). I want to reflect this character of holy, self-giving love into this groaning, strife-filled world.

One way I seek to do that is by publishing books that offer hope. I believe that hope is what sets "Christian books" apart among general book publishing. I agree with Madeleine L'Engle who said,

> And what is a 'Christian' book? Is it something that will be appreciated and understood only by Christians? Is it telling the Good News to those who already know it? Is it preaching to the choir? I want my books to bring joy and hope and courage, and I pray that they are and will be inclusive and not exclusive.[2]

A book is paper printed on and bound together into a volume for reading. Or a digital file stored in a computer database, an internet cloud, or hand-held device for reading on a screen. Or a recording of written material into sound bytes for listening. Books come in many forms. And there's nothing intrinsically "Christian" about the forms.

The person who envisions, experiences, writes, edits, and/or publishes a book, however, may certainly be a follower of Christ. And hopefully that book will be written from a mind that is being renewed, a mind that seeks to view the world as Jesus the living Word spoke of it and acted in and for it.

I haven't found a perfect book yet, or a perfect person. But I've known people whose lives ring true, and I've read books that ring true.

Whether fiction, nonfiction, memoir, or poetry; a story, essay, or poem may portray a context of, and show the results of, brokenness, sin, and conflict. At the same time it will also *show* (not just *tell* about) grace—that untameable, uncontrollable, uncontrolling but ever-flowing presence of God at work in, for, and with all creation.

Such writers and publishers seek to shine a ray of hope that gives readers renewed courage to reach deeper or reach out (or "up" if you prefer that symbolism) and take hold of the reaching hand of God.

If you are a published or hoping to be published writer, if you are considering self publishing, or if you are already publishing books through your own name, imprint, company, or nonprofit, I invite you on a journey with me to discover, discern, and re-affirm a creative, organic, adventurous view of writing and publishing ministry.

During Christian publishing's heyday in the late 20th and early 21st centuries, religious publishing houses sprang up and grew strong, profitable, and influential, way beyond the Bible, music, and curriculum publishers of the fifties and sixties. During the seventies Christian stores began to proliferate. Later, many Christian publishers and imprints were acquired by major New York publishing houses (for instance, Harper Collins took over Zondervan). That opened the door for religion titles to get into American Booksellers Association stores. "Religion" and "Christian" sections burgeoned in major bookstore chains and in some independent retailers. Then in 1995 Amazon launched into book sales. Soon after that, self publishing became more and more doable, respectable, and competitive. Then print-on-demand (POD) expanded and improved in quality, with PDFs offering "what you see is what you get" technology in transfer of files. Social media platforms gave opportunities for promotions; a crazy ride on swelling waves that promised so much—then crashed on the rocks—with attention and hopes soon drawn to the next, newest wave.

With Christian publishing integrated more and more into the general market, the Christian Booksellers Association eventually weakened and finally folded in 2019. According to *Publishers Weekly*, today no more than twenty percent of Christian titles are sold through Christian bookstores.

> Over the past twenty-five years, religion publishing has undergone massive consolidation, as well as a revolution in retailing. With the rise of the internet came the demise of thousands of religion bookstores and entrance to the mainstream market. Social change and challenges have prompted religious presses' attention to new voices among editors and writers, as well as the views of readers who are increasingly detached from traditional theology and church affiliation.[3]

Within a post-modern, increasingly pluralistic and secular society, and a divided political landscape, as churches re-evaluate what *ecclesia* means, many Christians are deconstructing and some are reconstructing their beliefs. A growing number of the population identifies as SBNR ("spiritual but not religious"). They include the "Nones" (no religious affiliation) and the "Dones" (those who have left organized church).[4] In this changing landscape how and what do we write and publish—especially in a sustainable way that will last and continue to grow and have influence?

In the following chapters, we consider five aspects of what I call organic publishing: *Soak, Spoke, Evoke, Provoke,* and *Stoke.* We need to ...

- SOAK (first ourselves and then our readers) in mentally, physically, socially, spiritually healthy nutrients, water, and life-sustaining soil.

- Listen to wise words and the Living Word SPOKEn through the ages and still speaking. Then use words ourselves with care and creativity.

- Write narratives to EVOKE the beautiful, good, and true, the transcendent within the imminent, to remind and re-enchant.

- PROVOKE with our writing, cultivating vision, action, and community for a future of healing, renewal, and wholeness.

- Continue to STOKE the fires of awareness, refinement, and relational engagement.

I choose the mindset of an under-gardener. My Father is the Gardener. Working with the Gardener, I purpose to dig, prepare the soil, and sow seeds with words. The resulting fruit may never fully be seen or measured. But I will seek to cultivate wheat, not chaff, and do it with love.

Now, if you'll excuse me, I will—like my farming forebears—lick my finger and hold it to the wind....

Chapter One
SOAK

"Mine was an imagination well-prepared for the invasion of the gospel story. The soil had been fertilized in my youth with a hundred tales that had taken root and grown but had born no fruit; those old stories withered, then decayed and composted, readying the ground for the life-giving seeds that were coming."
—Andrew Peterson

"Sometimes as a writer what is going on inside you must compost so that something else can come out. We don't just produce on demand. But something is brewing."
—Paul Kingsnorth

"God wants us to write—not for him or about him—but with him."
—Allen Arnold

My mother-in-law's motto was "Cleanliness is next to godliness." She didn't speak those words often, but she lived them. She admitted once to me, as she watched me enjoy my young children, that she wished she had spent more time playing and reading with her own children instead of constantly and fastidiously cleaning, dusting, and ironing. Dirt was not tolerated in the house. But, as a daughter of Danish dairy farmers, she knew the value of soil in its place, where it supported pasture for grazing and produced fields of root crops and hay for feed.

Is "dirt" a dirty word? Gossips and scandalmongers delight in sharing the "dirt" on neighbors. Tabloids dish out "dirt" on the rich and famous. Some people shudder at dirty jokes. Such uses of the word, though, obscure the value, the necessity, the preciousness of actual, living, breathing dirt.

In the gospels we read of Jesus spitting in dirt and applying the mud to a blind man's eyes. In the garden of Gethsemane, we are told, his sweat came like drops of blood that fell to the ground and mixed with the dirt (see Luke 22:44). In John 19:35 we read that on the cross Jesus' side was pierced by a sword and out came water and blood, no doubt running onto and soaking into, the rocky ground.

Dust—dry, easily blown away—has long been a symbol of death. Dusty dirt that has separated into particles lacks the cohesion of healthy soil. According to the Genesis account, we are created out of dust, and into this formed dust the Spirit of God breathes life.

Oxygen rich soil supports life. To "soak" soil in organic matter allows seeds to receive moisture and roots to receive nutrients for growth. Gardeners "soak" garden soil by adding organic matter such as compost to help it hold moisture, break up compacted areas of clay, give density to sandy areas, and encourage proliferation of beneficial organisms. This method develops rich humus and garden loam. Similarly, some vegetable seeds sprout faster and more reliably if they are first soaked in water before planting. To encourage germination, one can soak spring seeds to make them more ready to engage with, and respond to, the soil and sun.

Like soaking seeds before planting or soaking the ground before digging, the writer and publisher soaks in vision, prayer, learning, and community.

To soak means both 1) to penetrate or permeate and 2) to savor an experience. We may either "soak up" or "soak in." I have soaked in sunshine, a warm bath, in family gatherings/social togetherness, and in the presence of the Spirit as I pray, worship, contemplate, and walk in nature.

We, like dirt, aren't going to produce much good vegetation and fruit if we don't first allow ourselves to be dug, stirred, and rejuvenated. As writers and publishers, we soak in, and trust ourselves to, the vision for our art, work, mission, and ministry. We may soak in prayer and communion of our spirit with God's Spirit, desiring that Christ will enliven our words, actions, and presence. We want our books (and blogposts and podcasts) to contain seeds of life.

Our personal soaking involves assessing our time, talent, treasure, opportunity, experience, expertise, connections, education, and relationships. Do we have people around us for needed support, collaboration, and encouragement?

In what other contexts are we soaking? Each of us is soaked in a theological (and societal) stew, whether we give it thought or not. I think we should give it thought. Ask questions about the health of that stew. Know what you believe. Seek, study, and pray to sync your beliefs with your actions. Be open, though, to change and to understanding others' perspectives, experiences, traditions, and scriptural interpretations. When deciding what to write and publish, these things matter. They are essential.

Like it or not, we are deeply soaked in modernity. During the modern period the soil of creation/nature and human progress has been managed by a scientistic worldview that denies the sacredness of the soil. Great crops were grown, with huge yields, seemingly giving life to the world. But the soil of human souls became thin and depleted. Postmodernism is a reaction to that, and it has served to point out, with absurdity and cynicism, the weaknesses of modernity. Perhaps it has disturbed, begun the breaking up, of fallow ground. But postmodernism is still not nourishing the hunger of the human heart for depth and connection.

I have soaked in and soaked up the ethos of my history and wider culture. I grew out of American soil, planted here by parents with a heritage of Protestant faith and northern European ancestry. My English and Scots Irish forebears began arriving in the new world before the Revolution. Opportunity drew them. They settled, labored, and farmed in the colonies, then gradually migrated across the middle of the United States. The destinies of different family streams converged in Eastern Colorado, the area that James Michener wrote about so eloquently and convincingly in the novel Centennial. He portrayed the short grass prairie, with its rivers running down from, and its high plains and prairie rolling up to the Rocky Mountains as a center of natural and human history, a sequence of civilizations where landforms and ecosystems have developed, animal life and people groups have come and gone. A place where, in the grand scheme of historical eras, as the Pawnee Indians often repeated, "Only the rocks endure forever...."[5] Those towering granite peaks still preside over continual change.

My father told how his grandparents came to homestead in Colorado at the start of the twentieth century. As kids in a Nebraska town where Florabelle's family were English Methodists who looked askance at George's family of Scottish Presbyterians, the two young people fell in love. Determined young George looked westward. He traveled (by stagecoach, train, horse, or all three?) to Montana to herd sheep and earn enough money to marry his sweetheart. Crossing a corner of the young state of Colorado he must have seen the small, sod houses and square farm plots scattered among the open areas populated mostly by pronghorn, deer, fox, prairie dogs, and coyote. He saw opportunity. The young couple took the train as far as the line went (before the rails joined east and west with the golden spike in Utah). They packed their few belongings, including Florabelle's books—Bible, novels, and poetry—into a covered wagon and found their designated plot of wild prairie. As children were born and growing, Florabelle insisted that Sunday was as much a day of rest as hardworking homesteaders in an unforgiving land could manage, with Bible reading and family prayers. The pioneers had camp meetings in the summer and one-room schoolhouses for the children. But not yet a church or a secondary school.

One day an itinerant evangelist stopped by the homestead. He had a request: Could he use a corner of George's farm to set up a tent for holding revival services, with hopes of building and starting a church? The young denomination he represented believed God is holy love. George said it sounded good to him. Surely sovereign God is holy. Florabelle had been taught the Wesleyan view that "God is love." They chose to provide space for a revival tent. And they became charter members of the brand-new church.

I have inherited George's Bible. The Psalms contain the most worn pages, and the following verses (among others) are marked with pencil:

> His seed shall endure for ever, and his throne as the sun before me. It shall be established for ever as the moon, and as a faithful witness in heaven.... **Before the mountains were brought forth**, or ever thou hadst formed the earth and the world, even from everlasting to everlasting, thou art God. (emphasis mine)[6]

In revering the rocks rising high above the plains, did the Pawnee of Colorado intuitively "see" beyond that dependable source and solidity to the Rock that is Christ?

The hopeful, adventurous pioneers—whose feet walked westward, their hands worked the dry dirt, and their eyes watched the sky for moisture—staked their hopes in the land, God's vision and provision, the Bible, and community. They brought fragments of culture with them and they learned to watch for and create beauty. Their survival depended on rain coming, crops growing, and the neighbors' help. They always believed things would get better; they could give their children a brighter future if they worked hard, obeyed God, shared with others, sacrificed, saved, and—as in the case of Florabelle, my poetry-reading, piano-playing, flower-growing great grandma—kept dreaming.

I now possess hindsight that the hopeful pioneers and immigrants didn't have, as my grandchildren are now viewing the era of my youth with fresh perspective. In my youth, all institutions were called into question. Yes, many teenagers and young adults were sincerely rebelling against unjust systems, but many others were riding along for the trippiness of turning on, tuning in, and dropping out.

In my grandparents' day, churches, the Bible, and ministers generally held places of respect and authority in people's lives, though many denominations began splintering and offshoots developed over differences of interpretations, dogmas, and practices. Was something new beginning to emerge? Author and publisher Phyllis Tickle described this era thus:

> North American Christianity entered into the time of emergence already possessed of some relative difference of opinion about where authority lies. [Conservatives and Social Justice Christians] are quite clear that *sola scriptura, scriptura sola* is indeed the foundational source from which all authority flows. [Liturgicals and Renewalists] are not so sure, however.[7]

The churches in California, where I grew up and lived most of my life, had felt the impact of the Dust Bowl migration, the post-war Baby Boom, the Cold War, increasingly secular public education, and growing multi-culturalism. Fear was a great motivator, even while society retained the modern mindset of, and trust in "progress." Sunday Schools flourished as townspeople happily let their children go on church busses Sunday mornings. There was still a basic trust in the church and basic folk knowledge of the Bible and Jesus. But that was gradually changing. Tickle credits the automobile, more free time, and the birth control pill for making many of the changes possible. But during the 50s and 60s, when in trouble, people still turned to the church. When I was a young child, needy and desperate people still showed up regularly at our parsonage door seeking help from the preacher and his wife.

By the final decades of the twentieth century, especially in the north Bay Area where my husband and I lived and raised our children, the increasingly secular population seemed to think the church was not a place to which they could turn and get help. They turned instead to AA, sensitivity groups, New Age retreats, Buddhist practices, transcendental meditation, choosing to be "spiritual but not religious."

The case had been clearly made that the journey of the spirit did not require the baggage of religion to be a worthy and rewarding trek.[8]

In the wake of these trends, those churches that proved to be places people could and did get help, thrived. These churches were willing to get their hands dirty working the soil (you might say), searching for tap roots, digging wells, testing the wind, planting seeds in season and out, expecting showers and rejoicing when the "spiritual," soaking rains came.

During the late twentieth century, we saw missions come to America. Other-language congregations shared our buildings, and we sponsored refugees. I remember when, in the late 1990s, we whites became the "majority minority" in California. We Americans who had brought Western European culture and "conquered" the new world, caught more than were taught the idea that we were a city on a hill founded to bless the world and to "civilize the heathen." We had sacrificially supported foreign missions. Now we were visited by preachers from other lands coming to tell us about fresh experiences of God. They were glad to receive our financial help. But what they brought to us was better than anything money could buy.

Though some voices are now declaring the end of Christendom, Christianity continues to grow in the Southern hemisphere. What are we in the global north, then, to do? How do we go forward as followers of Jesus and as leaders of ministries? Various options are proposed from different corners:

- Rod Dreher, a Protestant convert to Catholicism then Eastern Orthodoxy, in *The Benedict Option* [9] calls for a new monasticism conserving the authority of religious and family traditions.

- A surprising number of evangelical Protestants are converting to Roman Catholicism, seeking apostolic authority for their faith and lives (famous recent example: Mark Galli, former editor of *Christianity Today*). Catholic evangelist Bishop Robert Barron and contemplative Fransciscan Richard Rohr, engage often and deeply in dialog with Protestants of past and present, and have wide influence.
- Numerous young men, especially, are moving from Protestant to Eastern Orthodox. Influential examples are Canadians Jonathan Pageau and Bradley Jersak.
- Many evangelicals are digging in their heels and holding to literalism and exceptionalism, even falling prey to conspiracy theories, fear of change, and fear of the future.
- Liberal and progressive Christians are looking to the edges, to those who have been marginalized, making inclusivity their priority (perhaps partly in reaction to the previous group mentioned?).
- Some are responding to the moment by seeking to create a "big tent." A hospitable church rooted in biblical, historic Christianity, with the practice of truth (not necessarily fact), of goodness (not necessarily the only "right"), and of beauty (that engages all the senses as well as the spirit).
- Many are deconstructing their faith. Hopefully they will reconstruct in healthy ways. They are leaving traditional, organized church and either "going to church" online or seeking community elsewhere, such as in nature or in pub gatherings.

Varieties of, and need for, change in American religious life in the twentieth century were described in 1985 in *Habits of the Heart*. In their attempt to understand how religion influences American society, Robert N. Bellah, et.al., utilized Ernst Troeltsch's three types of religious community: Church, Sect, and Mysticism:

> Whereas the church enters into the world culturally and socially in order to influence it, the sect stands apart from the secular world, which it sees as too sinful to influence except from without. ...'mysticism' is one in which the focus is on the spiritual discipline of the individual however he or she relates to the world.[10]

Within this model, my spiritual roots grew to some extent in all three types of religious soil. Now as I look back and analyze those roots, I can recognize three patterns:

1. Christians have had difficulty clearly defining and understanding what Scripture, tradition, and history mean by "the world." Church, Sect, and Mysticism each define "the world" in slightly different ways that make a big difference in how they believe, live, and practice their faith (and make a big difference in the mindset and activity of faith-based writers and publishers).

2. Each of these three types of religious community, Church, Sect, and Mysticism, distinguishes and integrates head religion and heart religion differently and to different effect.

3. The 'good ol' American value' of individualism plays out differently in each: Church, Sect, and Mysticism.

As I first wrote this chapter, the Covid-19 Pandemic restrictions were lifting as attention moved to Russia's invasion of the Ukraine, and to a new election cycle in the U.S. Our divisions grow ever more pronounced. Voices call for leaving behind Christendom, modernism, scientism, dogmatism, and instead seeking experience of the Spirit, seeking meaning in the chaos and a "re-enchantment" of this world. Tickle also spoke to such human yearnings:

> The duty, the challenge, the joy and excitement of the Church and for the Christians who compose her, then, is in discovering what it means to believe that the kingdom of God is within one and in understanding that one is thereby a pulsating, vibrating bit in a much grander network.[11]

In our postmodern context, the emerging church is a conversation—relational, radical, and interconnected, pulsating with the excitement of expanding spiritual horizons. I think the pandemic, for those who were open, sped up the desire for the mystical, as well as the distrust of authority and meta-narrative. But, as Tickle continues,

> Narrative, on the other hand, is the song of the vibrating network. ... [It] circumvents logic, speaking the truth of the people who have been and of whom we are. Narrative speaks to the heart in order that the heart, so tutored, may direct and inform the mind.[12]

Diana Butler Bass, in *Grounded*, adds to the conversation:

> Recent decades ... have slowly illuminated that an intimate presence of mystery abides with the world, a spirit of compassion that breathes **hope and healing**.

And with it, faith is shifting from a theology of distance toward a theology of nearness, **from institution to unmediated experience**. (bolding is mine)[13]

Is this unmediated experience what my great grandparents intuited as they worked the earth, watched the sky, rejoiced in, collected, and carefully used precious water? They could see long distances out on those vast plains under blue skies. Toward the eastern horizon they remembered family and traditions and places they had left, but which they certainly carried inside themselves. Toward the western horizon they glimpsed the alpine peaks from whence the rivers flow, and beyond that the Pacific Coast (where our family's westward expansion would stop and then start migrating back eastward). But what fed them daily was the kitchen garden. Here's Bass again:

> And that, of course, is another vision of heaven: a garden. Where dirt, water, and air all come together to feed us, to heal the earth, to produce the atmosphere we need to survive. Paradise, really. Here and now.[14]

When we respect, depend on, and work with dirt, water, air—we sense the power inherent in creation. In the West, we experience periodic and episodic droughts, floods, fires, windstorms, earthquakes. We roll with it (literally, during earthquakes!). But we keep hoping, healing, and rebuilding. Similarly, cultural storms rock the church. William Abraham's words speak here, especially to Christian evangelicals:

> If in the process we continue to hold that we can somehow redeem the evangelical experiment without **divine grace**, then we have only ourselves to blame. We can break up the ground, tear up the weeds, plant seeds of truth, fence out the wild animals, and share our

dreams of the ultimate landscape. We cannot of ourselves either fully predict the outcome or control the secrets of life and growth." (bolding is mine)[15]

Brian McClaren adds,

> No wonder so many religious folks today wear down, burn out, and opt out.... And no wonder more and more of us who are Christians by birth, by choice, or both, find ourselves shaking our heads and asking, 'What happened to Christianity? What happened to Jesus and his beautiful message?'[16]

As institutions change, which they have done throughout history, I keep remembering the Pawnee refrain, "Only the rocks endure forever."

Christ is the Rock, and Christ's body the church in the world will endure.

And what does all this mean for my small, faith-based writing and publishing ministry (and perhaps yours)? Let me share a few insights with you.

First, soak in the knowledge that you are part of something far bigger than yourself. The communion of saints. The body of Christ. The continual joining of heaven and earth. The interconnectedness of, and ongoing creation of, all things. Soak in words, in poetic expression, in beauty. Soak in the call, the vision, the desire of God. Soak in learning from the experience of wise others. Let all these things refresh and enliven the soil of your mind and heart like long-awaited spring rain.

Like gardeners sifting compost through a screen to remove hard chunks, so we sift the past to incorporate it into our future, into what we are becoming. Much of our past may not be compostable into nutritious mulch by which to build a future or to become new. Jesus said, "Behold, I make all things new." As has been said, "We can't change the past, but we can change our relationship to the past."

Next, with discernment soak your thinking and experience in the context around you. Listen to the earth, the wind, the tenor of people's talk, the hunger for meaning and purpose and courage. Write and publish what brings together heaven and earth, the immanent and the transcendent, individuals and community. Ask questions, be curious, strive to understand various positions and perspectives.

We can become soaked to the point of sogginess in abstract thought and propositional concepts of creation, sin, grace, salvation, the church age, and eschatology. We need to let some of the abstract drain out of our spongy minds, then choose to soak ourselves in embodied experiences of—through contact with—those who constitute the "rocky," "shallow," "dry," and "thorny" soils as well as the "prepared" soils of Jesus' parable: the marginalized, forgotten, and neglected. Listen to them. This will keep us grounded.

An effective minister who pastors a congregation will move out into the context of the people, their workplaces, their homes and families, their events such as games and concerts, their hospital bedsides. That's being grounded in a way that the Spirit can be present and manifest. Similarly, the person who writes and publishes books will get to know their readers' joys and trials and will not come into their presence through what they have written in a book, convinced of the certain, final answers; will not speak/preach/write expecting all to listen, assuming all will be helped if they just take heed. True communication doesn't work that way. Being transformed by the renewing of the mind requires soaking in community, relationships, corporate embodied worship, communion, and dialog. That's a challenge for a book and a reader to accomplish together. How does that happen?

The dailiness of the communication task is overwhelming.

If only we could get away for a while to some quiet, sacred place and find rest, renewal, and transformation. Surely, then, our writing, as well as our lives, could be revolutionized.

But our lives are so daily, made of moments piled upon moments, experiences both planned and unexpected. Perhaps, though, your daily routine includes habits that you don't even view as being "spiritual exercises" but that can gradually give the perspective you crave. That was the case for me.

Finally, remember: to speak *to* the hearts of others, we must speak *from* the heart. But first we must get in touch with our own hearts. Jesus said, "out of the abundance of the heart the mouth speaks." If you want the words that flow out of your mouth or pen to be purposeful, meaningful, life giving ... then first tend to your inner life. But how? In his book, *Pray, Write, Grow: Cultivating Prayer and Writing Together*, Ed Cyzewski describes his practice of daily self reflection that "grew into an essential exercise that also revolutionized my writing."[17]

A few years ago, I, myself, felt overwhelmed and pulled in various directions by duties, desires, and demands. I longed for focus and clarity, an unbroken sense of the Lord's presence, and a new release of creativity. At bedtime I found myself thinking back over my day, and I focused my mind on the best thing that happened that day: the time during that day when I felt the most joy and life. I saw those moments as gifts and drifted to sleep embracing the gift God had given me that day:

- a child's laughter
- sunlight dancing on a pond
- flowers blooming in my garden
- a surprise visit or card from a friend
- the way the Lord spoke to me through a scripture and came close to me in prayer

- the way the phrases, rhythms, and rhymes of a poem I was composing came together.

These moments I treasured in my heart. They gave me hope and a sense of anticipation for the next day, to see what the next day's moments would bring.

Then I found a charming little book by Linn and Linn, *Sleeping With Bread: Holding What Gives You Life*,[18] and I learned that what I was doing was a type of Christian spiritual practice called "the Examen," taught by the Jesuits and rooted in the writings of St. Ignatius who invites us to find God in all things by reflecting prayerfully back on a day (or a week, a year) and asking, "What today gave me consolation and life?" One also may ask, "What took life from me, gave me a feeling of desolation?"

It is good for the soul to embrace and hold to the life-giving, consoling moments of our days. And over time, we can observe patterns and learn what we can best focus our energies on, because God indeed speaks to us through the experiences of our days; God wants us to experience life and joy and consolation in a way that will flow out of us to others.

As Christian writers and publishers, rather than laboring to publish words and thoughts we think we *ought* to write, or that others seem to expect; we can instead write the forms, subjects, themes, and styles that engage and express our hearts as well as our minds, that fill us with consolation, hope, joy, and life. Then, most likely the resulting piece will do the same for our readers.

On the first day of June one year, my husband, Larry, and I decided to get clear away from office, computers, books, and other projects. We felt a hankering for bird watching and wildflower viewing. So, we drove out to the Pawnee National Grassland, bringing our dog Jasper with us. This protected habitat on the high, short-grass prairie of

Northeastern Colorado provides nesting ground to a colorful variety of migratory birds as well as other native wildlife.

Some years the grassland—a vast solitude under changing skies—is hot and dry. This time after a wet spring, we found it cool and green. Wildflowers dotted the native grasses. Prickly Pear were opening their blooms. And the birds! They foraged in the grasses, perched on fence posts, did aerial gymnastics to catch flying insects, scratched in the sandy roadside, hunted from the sky, and paddled on small ponds.

We identified twenty-five bird species, including Vesper Sparrow, Prairie Falcon, and Loggerhead Shrike. At one point along the gravel road, we spotted a bird that looked like a miniature roadrunner. It ran on the ground with its tail held high. We watched it through binoculars and checked our bird guide (and the birding app on my cell phone, the only technology we used that day). It appeared to be a Sage Thrasher. Then the bird lifted into the air and we thought our chance to observe it was over. But it landed on a fence post just ahead of where we had stopped our car on the narrow road.

As the breeze ruffled its feathers, the Sage Thrasher lifted its head and sang! And sang and sang. What a show. It felt like a gift to have this bird—uncommon in our area—perch and sing for us. In the wonder of this bird perching and singing so close to us, we felt even more connected with nature around us.

This emotional and spiritual connection is important. We connect with people, share ideas, express creativity, and conduct business through keyboard, screen, digital images and sounds, artificial light and wi-fi connection. This virtual world is full of potential and offers fascination. But experiencing life through technology can gradually drain our souls. One way I know this soul drain is happening is, when I go to bed, close my eyes and, instead of drifting to a peaceful sleep, I see images and text, web pages and video flashing across the screen of my mind. (This is why I generally turn off my computer by 9:30-10:00 p.m.)

King David declared, "He leads me in green pastures and beside still waters. He restores my soul."[19] Occasionally we need to unplug, go out into a world that engages all the senses, and let our souls be restored. Nature and the rediscovery of wonder offer a gateway to a restored soul. Carol O'Casey, author of *Unwrapping Wonder*, writes,

> I escape expectations ... and take a walk on the wild side. Whether exploring field or forest, marsh or meadow, or the edge of the sea, in the natural world I am transformed. There, in the solitude of nature I experience God's presence.[20]

That night, after a day of birding on the prairie, when I lay my head on the pillow, I began to realize what a gift I had brought home with me from the grassland. When I closed my eyes, my mind wasn't filled with a screen through which virtual images came at me. No. Instead, I was still among the Lark Buntings, Horned Larks, and Longspurs winging, swooping, twirling in the air. I was still surrounded by the songs of Meadow Larks, Brown Thrashers, and Mountain Plovers. I was still watching Swainson's Hawks soar on high and kite in the breezes. I was still enjoying the yellow, blue, and red wildflowers and smelling the sweet grasses. With these images, sounds and smells came a peaceful, delighted, and deep sense of Presence—of our Creator, the Restorer of our souls.

If writing and connecting with readers (to encourage them, lift their sights to Jesus, come alongside them to encourage, instruct, and inspire, to bring them hope and insight through a well-told story) is what gives you life ... then this may be what God is calling you to do. About this holy calling prolific Christian author Bruce Epperly says,

> As a writer, I see my work as a holy task, reflecting divine inspiration in my finite and fallible experience. ... I don't claim to be a conduit for God's wisdom: I recognize that in this dynamic of call and response, I am the one who is ultimately responsible for the quality and insight of my writing. I believe that writing is a way of responding to divine inspiration for the good of others. In fact, I see my writing as creatively shaping the lives of those around me, providing inspirational, provocative, and healing possibilities.[21]

We easily look out at the world to find "what's the matter with things." But if we want God to "touch each moment with insight," it's important to occasionally look within. We need springtimes in our souls. In early spring we prepare gardens by digging. My young son read to me a riddle once: "What keeps getting bigger and bigger the more you take away from it?" The answer? "A hole." I could just as well answer, "My heart."

"Break up your fallow ground, and sow not among thorns" (Jer. 4:3). If we respond willingly to this call, the Spirit will help us spade rocks and stubborn roots out of our hearts: attitudes, frustrations, fears, doubts, resentments, irritations. It may hurt. But to feel the Gardener close is worth it. The Master Gardener "takes out the heart of stone and gives us a heart of flesh (Ez. 36:26). If we have allowed rubbish in our heart's soil—placed there by others or by ourselves—it poisons the soil and robs nutrients.

This heart renovation may require confession, repentance, starting new habits and practices, finding healthy community; and it may require counseling or therapy. God says to us, "Behold, I am for you, I am turning to you to till you and sow you" (Ez 36:9). As waters rise in our hearts, trees will flourish and bring nourishment, shelter, and healing to those around us, to those who read us. May it be so!

We don't need to fear this breaking up of our fallow ground. If a stone or hard place appears, we can release it. The more the Gardener takes away, the larger our hearts become!

Let yourself soak in the life of Christ. Then "go out" empowered to soak the soil around you in words that speak of that Life, convince of that Life, make ready for the seeds of that Life.

Chapter Two

SPOKE

"Words connect us to the 'long conversation' and to those who have given them life in prayers, poems, position papers, political documents, encyclicals, laws, and letters."
—Marilyn McEntyre

"The habit, very prevalent today, of dismissing words as 'just words' takes no account of their power."
—Dorothy Sayers

"I believed, and so I spoke ..."
—2 Cor. 4:13

In the beginning the Word issued from the Father calling forth order and beauty and goodness out of chaos. The Word continues to resonate, vibrating and longing and delighting. It speaks in and through all nature, it sings in the wind and the waves, in the awakening of life in springtime, in the bounty and provision of harvest, in the whispering silence of winter. It speaks of life and hope and presence from beyond and within.

This Word, this reality that is more real than our personal perceived realities, keeps erupting like a geyser, igniting like flame, and surprising us like flowers in the desert. The Word is Beauty sung by the stars, chanted by the birds, and celebrated by the seasons. The Word is Truth ever unfolding, rescuing loose ends and weaving them into the tapestry of creation and new creation. The Word is everlastingly, dependably, patiently Good.

Best of all, the Word has appeared to us, has come into our milieu, has joined with us in our earthiness, has incarnated, in a sense in all creation, and especially in the person of Jesus. The Word has been spoken, written, and published on stone tablets and on hearts.

Jesus, a historical person—yet so much more. God incarnate revealed to us in human form, pointing out birds and flowers and rocks, touching untouchables, healing the sick, listening to outcasts, laughing with children, hanging on a cross, wearing a crown of thorns, providing a door—a way—to God and godlikeness.

What have we done with this Jesus? The church, the community of believers in Jesus, today, it seems to me, is like a patchwork quilt, with a myriad randomly shaped pieces sewn together. Each is kept unique and separate by carefully and tightly stitched borders. Each believes their little patch is the center of the quilt with all the truth that is needed through which the story, the Word, must speak and be heard. One piece of the quilt is shaped like personal holiness, another has the shape of God's sovereignty, another of the great commission, another of care for the poor, another of social transformation, another of God's law, another of miracles, another of liturgy.

Each is a piece. Each has received blessings from God. Each defends their statements of faith, their requirements for membership, and their interpretations of holy scripture; their traditions, doctrines, and dogmas as sacred and sacrosanct. However, I wonder: is each "piece" in the patchwork lacking life-giving fibers that are meant to be threaded throughout the entire "quilt"?

Perhaps this "crazy quilt" has missed the mark of its true, intended form. Perhaps it is meant to be a tapestry. Perhaps it could be, and will be, transformed into an interwoven design that will resound with an all-encompassing celebration of the Word in all its facets and ramifications. What if we allowed our tightly-stitched border seams to be released and pulled and stretched across boundaries to work into the pattern of other pieces, giving here, receiving there, interacting, interplaying, cooperating with the Artist, until the craziness (and what may appear to be chaos) is transformed into a meaningful, purposeful, beautiful, winsome, out-reaching, in-gathering, whole.

When the golden and silvery threads meant to be woven throughout the whole church are freed to work their pattern and creativity, they will reveal the God who is both Spirit and Love. When this tapestry will be viewed from different angles and in different light, the many aspects of the Christ will shine and speak forth. Souls who have been wandering and dangling on the frayed edges will be able to see in the tapestry a revelation of Jesus—exactly what—Who—they need. Eventually they may surely, willingly, healingly join the torn, unraveled fabric of their lives with the tapestry of Life.

One could also describe a patchwork of small farms. Each wants to keep out the invasive weeds, possible toxic chemicals, and unwanted seeds of neighboring fields. Those with water rights don't want others using their resources. They don't want their crops hybridizing with those of the neighbors. Purity, profit, and production are their priorities.

As organic writers and publishers, where do we each fit in these pictures? Are we bounded or centered? If bounded, then what are our boundaries protecting? If centered, on what are we centered? This concept was explained by Phyllis Tickle in *The Great Emergence*. She says rather than the terms *centered* and *bounded,* more commonly today we hear "believe-behave-belong" as compared to "belong-behave-believe."

This concept is illustrated by a story Robert Barron tells:

> There is a wonderful story told of a young man named Gregory, who came to the great Origen of Alexandria in order to learn the fundamentals of Christian doctrine. Origen said to him, 'First come and share the life of our community, and then you will understand our dogma.' The youthful Gregory took that advice, and he came in time to embrace the Christian faith in its fullness.... Something of the same impulse lay behind Gerard Manley Hopkins' word to a confrere who was struggling to accept the truths of Christianity. [He] did not instruct his

colleague by saying 'Read this book' or 'Consult this argument,' but rather, 'Give alms.' The living of the Christian thing has persuasive power.²²

That's why I like to publish books showing people living "the Christian thing."

The bounded set (or "believe-behave-belong") applies to traditional Roman Catholicism and historic Protestantism alike. It requires adherence to certain rules of doctrinal belief and human conduct as prerequisites to membership. In contrast, in the centered set (or "belong-behave-believe") one may simply belong to a gathering of Christians by virtue of a shared humanity and affinity. Association may lead to conviction and desire to behave like, and participate in practices of the group, which begins to shape belief.

I think the above observations by Barron and Tickle apply to Christian publishers. Denominational publishing houses will be more bounded. Small, Indie presses like mine can operate in a more centered fashion. While I don't require from authors a statement of faith or subscription to certain dogmas, I do want golden and silvery threads of the Living Word to weave through the written words of authors I publish. My stated purpose for Cladach Publishing from the beginning has been to publish books that show God at work in our world and people getting involved, working with God. In the process, I have published books by authors who are Nazarene, Baptist, Independent, Pentecostal, Reformed, Roman Catholic, Orthodox, Salvation Army, Anglican, and Evangelical.

I would go so far as to say that book publishing has and will continue to open, join, and interweave threads of various streams, traditions, and patches of Christian teaching and practice; and to engage in conversation with other traditions in a pluralistic society.

For decades now, since the beginning of the Christian

publishing phenomenon, religious books have expanded as a book-publishing and book-selling category. And those religious books have reached across denominational bounds, blurring some theological distinctions in the pews and in the popular mind.

Books written by Christian men and women well known for their parachurch, megachurch, and media leadership and presence are studied in groups across denominational lines. They are quoted in pulpits in many if not most denominations. Some critics would say this trend has watered down distinctive theologies and doctrines. Others would say this trend is part of a process of newness emerging. Still others would point out the need for authoritative sources and voices and structures. Is something true because a well-known author published it in their book? How important is apostolic authority? Ancient texts and liturgies? The Church Fathers? The Mystics? Confessions of Faith? Historic Christian Creeds? Input from science and influence of cultures? Fundamentals and Essentials of the Faith?

In an attempt to "get people saved," are we simply feeding people the words we think they must believe and subscribe to? Or do we teach, guide, invite readers into a relationship of walking with, listening to, and learning to know the God who is Love and the Lord who speaks in parables? Do we teach information about biblical characters and historical believers as precepts? Or do we share narratives that invite and encourage our readers to walk with and encounter the living God themselves? Does our authority as communicators lie in our certainty and complete understanding? In a wider culture where modernity's clear-cut categories and dogmatism are being eschewed in favor of paradox, irony, and "both-and" thinking, in order to communicate effectively, we need to pay attention to emergent thinking that is more mystical, subtle, and unafraid of paradox. We can do this, not so much through propositions, but through narrative, storytelling. Reach minds via hearts.

> Narrative circumvents logic, speaking the truth of the people who have been and of whom we are. Narrative speaks to the heart in order that the heart, so tutored, may direct and inform the mind.[23]

We need to open our ears, dig deep, tune our hearts to hear the songs of creation, the stories of heaven coming to earth, of earth reaching for heaven, words of the heart, narratives of the soul. If we don't want to just "preach to the choir" but hope to speak into a postmodern world, we will not shy from mysticism, paradox, and irony. Jesus didn't. For instance, in Matthew's gospel Jesus says, "For those who want to save their life will lose it, and those who lose their life for my sake will find it" (Matt. 16:25). And also, let me remind you that we Christians hold to the paradoxical teaching that the Kingdom of God is now *and* not yet!

Trusting God to work through us, living incarnationally, desiring to reach people soaked in postmodernism, Christian communicators would do well to adopt the following practices and mindsets:

- Don't speak/write as if you have the final word on a subject.
- Invite conversation. Engage with good faith. Bring in other viewpoints.
- Emphasize experience and narrative. Share your story.
- Feel free to juxtapose disparate and surprising elements.

- Embrace irony and accept and enjoy paradox.
- Live and work in an attitude of hospitality.
- Ask honest questions. Consider no question out of bounds.
- Eschew pat or final answers.

One young Christian artist and poet, was asked on Twitter (now X), "What, in your opinion, is the state of Christian art?" She answered,

> As Madeleine E'ngle said, 'If it's bad art, it's bad religion, no matter how pious the subject.' I think there is a resurgence of talented and sincere artists of faith; [however], their subject matter might be more subtle than what is thought of as 'Christian.'[24]

The Word became flesh. Let *our words* be enfleshed. Embody the old, ever new story, in new contexts, metaphors, with imagination. Let *the Word* burst out of our carefully stitched seams. Let Creativity break through the protective boundaries.

I am encouraged when I hear young people today striving for a deeper sense of meaning, connection, and truth. They want something that will give them hope again. May they find the golden threads and follow them through the whole pattern that reveals the Christ Incarnate until the patchwork crazy quilt transforms into a pulsating, light-reflecting tapestry of Life and Love.

Whenever I sew, I end up using a seam ripper at some point to remove obstructive, crooked, or misplaced stitches. What are our tools—our seam rippers as writers and publishers? We stitch with words. We also rip with words.

I first experienced the wonder, the mystery, the call of

words as a very young child. Books were shuttered windows that opened new vistas; locked treasure boxes to open, holding keys to secret gardens; telescopes that brought the far and distant, even the eternal, into my imagination.

Books, those tantalizing tomes, held my preacher father's attention for hours but were mysteries to me. I wanted to read books myself. Then I wanted to write words like those in the books. I puzzled over how books came to be. How did all those words come together into evenly spaced lines and marks that made sense, that brought stories to life?

I encountered the mystery of layers of meanings of words, sensing nuance, even in the way my parents used words, with chuckles and winks and some hidden communication passing between them that told me the words they were saying held innuendos and connotations that I didn't yet know. I wanted to know!

School teachers taught me to print letters of the alphabet in neat, separate blocks that stood up straight and walked on the lines. I loved practicing cursive in fourth grade, copying the shape and slant of letters, feeling that deeper mysteries were opening to me, along with the mystery of self expression. The words somehow felt as if they were flowing from within me but at the same time were connected to something distinctly outside of me. That was the greatest mystery yet! And it's one I continue to experience and explore.

Later I learned about etymology of words, using words concisely to express the concrete or the abstract. I learned to love and respect words, to use them, but take care not to abuse them. Writers like to play with words, but also take them seriously. We cherish them, listen to them, pray over them, wrestle with them, trust them, and are willing to release them, like grown children, into a world, a reading public, that may not understand them, may misinterpret and misquote them. But also may be enlightened, encouraged, emboldened by them. The well-chosen, correctly used, creatively connected, ingeniously employed word has power. A piece of writing that is Christ-infused, Christ-honoring can be Christ-giving to a world that needs the seed of the living Word.

With these building blocks of our stories, articles, blog posts, tweets, and books, we instruct, entertain, encourage, and influence. Words matter because they enable us to see the unseen, to know the unknowable, to grasp the unimagined.

Practically being raised on a church pew helped launch me on a literary path. We sang with gusto the gospel song, "Publish glad tidings, tidings of peace; tidings of Jesus, redemption and release." During my growing-up years as a pastor's daughter, as I watched my father and my mother minister in churches, I learned:

1. The potency and potential of words in a book

In those days, we were people of two books: the Bible and the hymnal. Every church service began and ended with opening that wondrous, substantial book, and often we held it up to share with the person next to us. The hymnal united the congregation as we joined our voices in lilting melodies and straightforward harmonies accompanied by my mother's lively piano playing, often eliciting "amens" of blessing. (I'm not being nostalgic here. I like the way we now stand in worship and look forward and upward together, often with lyrics projected on a screen.) All the symbols to help us make music together, though, resided on the pages of a book, all the words to elicit such response, blended in heart-stirring, mind-engaging, and soul-satisfying rhythm, sense, and rhyme.

In every church meeting the Bible was also opened—

and revered. The congregation stood for "the reading of the Word." With a reverent, sonorous voice, the preacher read a passage from the Bible, then exhorted from its inexhaustible storehouse of truth, wisdom, and life application. I saw evangelists hold their big, black leather Bibles aloft in one large hand while exclaiming something like, "The Word of God is alive! It is sharper than any two-edged sword, piercing enough to reveal your sin." And I quaked. But I also learned, quite young, that real comfort could be experienced from those pages. No mere words on paper. But alive! Jumping off the page and into the mind and heart of the reader or the listener. Quickening words!

2. The joy of writing, printing, disseminating words on paper

I watched my preacher father as he typed the church bulletin—and perhaps a newsletter—during the week on his old black typewriter (how I loved the clicking of the keys and how the little hammers hit the paper, resulting in words appearing and forming themselves into sentences that said something, and that people would read and use to plan their week). On Saturday Daddy would crank out maybe one- or two-hundred copies with his mimeograph machine. I can still smell the ink and hear the sheets of paper swoosh round the rollers and shoot out onto the pile of materials ready to be folded and stacked, then handed out and read—to inform and influence—to be published!

3. The importance of getting the word out

Twice a year our churches held extended revival services with an itinerant evangelist, and, in preparation, Daddy would mimeograph a flyer about the upcoming week of meetings. I remember a few times when he paid my sister and me 5¢ each per city block to take the flyers door-to-door and invite people to the services (though "city block" doesn't quite describe neighborhoods in these rural towns surrounded by farms). My sister and I learned the importance of overcoming our trepidation, knocking on doors, and getting out the word (much like the publicity side of book publishing).

4. The value of reading and sharing books

We had few toys (we played outside a lot) and TV (which we got when I was about 11) was our only "tech" entertainment. But always there were books. Books lined the shelves in my father's study. He took my sister and me to the public library regularly, encouraging us to browse and check out books that interested us. My sister read every horse book she could find, especially novels by Walter Farley. I read all the Louisa May Alcott books. And when we brought books home from school or library, our mother often read them, too, and we all enjoyed discussing together the stories. In fact, my sister and I always told each other the stories we read. As a result, I felt I'd read the *Black Stallion* books even though I never did. And she knew the characters and plots in *Little Women* and *Under the Lilacs* even though she didn't read them. She didn't have to. That ability to vicariously experience the stories really helped, because there were so many more books to discover! (A side note: As a young girl I'd hear people argue their point in conversation by saying, "Well, I know it's true. I read it in a book!" Whether people were readers or not, I observed, most had a sort of reverential awe of books.)

The Sound of Silence

Too many words, however, can simply add to the psychic noise and clutter. Noted writer, editor, and literary critic William Zinsser wrote,

Clutter is the disease of American writing. We are a society strangling in unnecessary words, circular constructions, pompous frills, and meaningless jargon.[25]

"Silence is golden," declared an old popular song. In Rocky Mountain National Park, at one of the many dazzling views of snow-capped peaks stands an interpretive sign with a quote from Andre Kostelantez (1955):

One of the greatest sounds of them all—and to me it is a sound—is utter, complete silence.

Because we live near it, I have visited this national park during all seasons. In spring and summer, the melodies of birds, squirrels, and chipmunks rise and fall on the air. In late summer and early fall, rutting elk calls bugle through the park. Then, on many winter days a soft, white, silent layer of snow quiets the scene. Would you think of this "utter, complete silence" as a sound, as Andre Kostelantez did—even "one of the greatest sounds of them all"?!

This question prompts further questions: Where/how do we find silence? Why is silence important and needed? What can we learn in silence? Do we tend to avoid—maybe even fear—silence?

Andre Kostelantez was a Jewish Russian immigrant to America who became one of the most successful conductors and arrangers of music in history. Among many accomplishments, he conducted the New York Philharmonic Orchestra.

I personally knew an orchestra musician who also spoke of silence as if it were a sound: She was my daughter's violin teacher. She drilled into my little daughter the concept that a "rest" in the music is an "important nothing."

Music rests, seasons of silence, "important nothings"; these provide natural, satisfying rhythms to music and to our lives. This principle is woven into creation. As physical, emotional, and spiritual beings, we need times of silence that can become "the greatest sound of all" to us.

In her memoir, *On Kitten Creek: Searching for the Sacred*, Nancy Swihart describes times of silence on the family farm:

> On prayer walks I do most of the listening. Up here in this sky-drenched pasture a comforting solitude is one of the greatest gifts the farm has provided—placing my body, soul, and spirit into the presence of God without distraction. [26]

Nancy has learned to embrace this life-enhancing principle, to seek and relish these important-nothing rest times that give meaning and lilt to the music of her life, ministry, and writing. We need to find ways to incorporate regular seasons of silence into the flow of our days.

Before humans had much writing, printing, or publishing, words were mostly spoken, person-to-person(s), in community. In our world today, most of the words we produce and consume are mediated through the printed page, and through audio/video/digital media. (Perhaps a media platform such as Youtube, though, is making it possible today for discursive language to encompass both the immediacy of spoken words with the lasting quality of written—or recorded—words.)

In spoken language we are given more clues to perceive what is being communicated: body language, facial expressions, intonation, inflection. With written language, we simply have words on a page, and with those we must evoke whole worlds of meaning. Words invoke mental images. Choose your words carefully.

My husband and I sometimes drive by a marshy field teeming with life. When our car speeds by, though, we miss the wildlife hidden in the grasses, wading in the mud, singing from the reeds. One day we stopped our car, rolled down windows; looked through binoculars; listened, smelled; felt and tasted the breezes. Myriads of bird life, colors, and textures of fauna and flora brought the place alive to us. Good writing does that also: draws in the reader, reveals hidden things, appeals to the senses, opens possibilities.

The following list gives most of the elements of style and "good writing" that I look for in a manuscript and strive for in the books I publish. These techniques give writing pizzazz so readers will want to invest in, engage with—be entertained, convinced, and inspired by—the writer's words. (We do want our writing to communicate as clearly and persuasively as possible.)

1. Write from your heart as well as your mind.
2. Write in the active voice. Choose strong, active verbs.
3. Write concretely, rather than abstractly. Show, don't just tell. Appeal to all the senses.
4. In nonfiction as well as fiction, use storytelling as much as possible.
5. Keep viewpoint(s) consistent.
6. Keep the reader's attention as each word, each sentence, each paragraph, each chapter leads to the next.
7. Maintain a logical or chronological flow of thought or action. Use transitions as needed.
8. Strive for precision and conciseness. Cut extraneous or repetitious words and phrases.

9. Give thought to word choices—consider subtleties, connotations, nuances.
10. Vary sentence structure and length.
11. Use your ear. Ask, do the sentences flow well? Does the dialog "sound" the way people talk?

The most effective authors have a burning desire to communicate through written expression and will pay the price to learn the craft of writing, will apply themselves to the process of writing, and will always keep their readers in mind. George Orwell described a scrupulous writer thus:

> In every sentence he writes he will ask himself at least four questions: What am I trying to say? What words will express it? What image or idiom will make it clearer? Is this image fresh enough to have an effect?[27]

An effective writer who is also a Christian, will love the Lord, love words, and love people. They can clearly answer these reporter's questions:

1. **Who**: They know for Whom and to whom they are writing.
2. **What**: They either have 1) a clear focus and plan for what they are writing or 2) are writing to "discover" what they believe, to think through a question or situation as they write.
3. **Where**: They have a place to write, a time to write, and have learned to snatch the moments and capture ideas as they come.
4. **When**: For this question, they would do well to repeat these words attributed to John Wesley: "If not now, when? If not me, who?"

5. **Why**: They know why they are writing. A writer's motives may vary: money (dream on), fame (rare and elusive), satisfaction, or "scratching the itch" because they can't not write. Or they relate to what Eric Liddell's character said in the movie *Chariots of Fire*: "God made me fast. And when I run, I feel his pleasure." As Christian author, Bruce Epperly paraphrases it, "God gave me words, and when I write I feel God's pleasure."[28]

Such a writer also has the potential to give pleasure to readers. Our writing, instead of feeding the reader the propositions and requirements of the life of faith, may draw the reader into community through our narratives; then, as the Spirit works, lead to behavior change and finally, to whole-hearted belief and commitment. In this way we are more likely to reach and influence readers immersed in a postmodern context.

Though Postmodernity has brought a moral ambiguity and relativity, religious voices have called us to consider postmodern claims, influences, and manifestations, and to ask ourselves how best to respond. Stanley J. Grenz states,

> Postmodernism is surely open to serious critique and has been challenged on a number of fronts …Christians must not fail in the end to engage postmodernism critically where that is required. At the same time, they must also be open to what postmodernism can teach us positively as a needed corrective to modernity…. Postmodernism poses certain dangers. Nevertheless, it would be ironic—indeed, it would be tragic—if evangelicals ended up as the last defenders of the now dying modernity. To reach people in the new postmodern context,

we must set ourselves to the task of deciphering the implications of postmodernism for the gospel.[29]

I recently heard a minister and writer say, "We can't change the past, but we can change our relationship to the past, and we can incorporate it into what we are becoming." Postmodernity feels like a transitional time of history when we sift the ancient truths, traditions, and practices for lasting seeds to bring into the newness God is always calling us toward. We are like farmers using new technology, equipment, and scientific understanding to plant, preserve, and grow legacy or heirloom seeds, then package and market them in fresh, new ways.

As we stand at this particular time in liminal space of the future's threshold, faith-based writers and publishers can (and I think must) find common ground for conversation with postmoderns through the following means:

1. Irony

During the past few decades of postmodernisms's strong influence on culture, through TV and other media viewers are bombarded with biting, sarcastic, ironic humor. But irony has long been a literary device. For instance, the Bible contains irony. I appreciate Jonathan Foster's contribution to this discussion when he says,

> Consider Saul having that 'Damascus experience,' where he realizes the thing he is persecuting is the very thing that could save him. Ironic, no? How could a writer incorporate that into their writing? How could they see that the things they fight against aren't necessarily the problems but the answer to their problems. Irony helps me find solutions right in the midst of the antagonism. How can writers help their stories lean into antagonism? A common

problem with 'Christian writing' and much of Christian theology is the tendency to pit good against bad in clear, lined-out ways, rather than see how the good and bad are mixed up together and how the divine is entangled within all of it.[30]

My husband and I like to watch British mysteries. A favorite series is *Inspector Lewis*. I especially like the very postmodern James Hathaway character, Lewis's young sergeant. He acts paradoxically, speaks with irony, and is an enigmatic person to those around him.

Hathaway seems to accept (though he struggles with it in himself) that good and bad are all mixed up together but to also recognize the face of God in each person encountered. Doubt and faith are mixed within him, but faith keeps rising.

Since he is a former Cambridge seminary student, people wonder why he chose to be a policeman instead of a priest. He's not preaching in a pulpit. But he is working for justice. And he is with people in their moments of greatest loss and felt needs. He doesn't always show the courteous respect to authority figures that is expected in the British heirarchical culture. But he offers his clean white handkerchief to a tearful woman. He sits and offers presence to bereaved and grieving loved ones of the murder victims. He can come across a bit arrogant in a taciturn way, bringing forth sometimes-pertinent bits of knowledge he has acquired with his superior intellect, in the depth and width of his Cambridge studies, and voracious reading. But he never brags about, and seldom makes known, his good deeds. For instance, when he takes a (rare) vacation, he tells Lewis that he is "meeting friends on an island." Lewis never learns all the facts, but viewers are shown a brief scene of Hathaway with a bunch of orphaned children at an island orphanage run by Catholic priests, where he is volunteering his time to paint the outside of the buildings.

Hathaway has evidently undergone a faith deconstruction. But Lewis, whose wife died in a hit-and-run, says he has lost his faith completely. In one brief scene toward the end of the series, the two are sipping their brew by a riverside in Oxford. As they observe the peaceful scene, birds singing and ducks floating on the sparkling current, Lewis gestures and comments, "What do we need God for when we have all this?!" Hathaway grins slightly and answers simply, "God is in everything."

In the last few episodes of the series, Hathaway suffers angst over his estrangement from his father who is fading, with dementia. His sister urges him to visit their father. He answers, "He won't even know I'm there." When Lewis tells him, "Go see your dad. Hold his hand," he answers, "We don't do holding hands." But he does go, sits with his father, reads to him, and, finally, even holds his hand. One wonders if he is mostly reading to himself when he reads Gerard Manley Hopkins' poem, "As Kingfishers Catch Fire," which includes these lines:

> *I say more: the just man justices;*
> *Keeps grace: that keeps all his goings graces;*
> *Acts in God's eye what in God's eye he is—*
> *Christ—for Christ plays in ten thousand places*
> *Lovely in limbs, and lovely in eyes not his*
> *To the Father through the features of men's faces.*

As he reads the last lines he gazes at his closed-eyed father toward whom he has found a measure of forgiveness and appreciation. Those viewers who "have ears to hear" will hear hints of the sacred. And so may our readers when we use similar narrative techniques in our writing.

The old saying "You can lead a horse to water but you

can't make him drink" is true for our readers. We might as well give up efforts to make people believe and start leading them gently and convincingly to living water—let them see that water, smell it, taste it, be enticed by it, and inch closer to it themselves.

2. Emphasis on Narrative

In postmodernism the relationship between words and images changes. The power of story as a moral reference point has superseded the didactic. Faith-based writers should not be put off by this. Don't we often hear, "Show, don't tell"? That's because, as postmoderns know, images speak with power that mere "preachy" words can't carry. And words can have different meanings to different people in different contexts. In fact, readers bring meaning to words. We writers work with the constant challenge of considering context and connotations, not just denotations, and of keeping possible perspectives of the reader in mind—all while "moving the story forward."

3. Playfulness

We Christians (including writers) can be so boringly serious! Have we forgotten how to play? Theologian Jürgen Moltmann defends play as meaningful, and as old as life itself.

> The genesis of the world and the order of everything in that world have the character of play.... It is only in play that human beings can endure the fundamental contingency of the world and adapt to that contingency.... Play is a symbol for the world which is also used for the world's redemption. Mystical theologians especially have used categories of play in ideas about the divine 'play of grace.'[31]

I love to think of God as actively creative in our world and in our lives, with a sort of give and take that could be called playful. Some theologies are more open to this idea than others, as author and theologian Jonathan Foster has found:

> Open and relational theology has really helped me emphasize and esteem the role of creativity (which might be a synonym for play). Alfred North Whitehead talks about how beauty is the harmonization of diversity. It's not the domination of diversity, but the harmonization. This takes a creative, playful approach. An approach that is 'at home' with discordant ideas, themes, metaphors, and story lines. An approach that weaves the discordant idea into a larger idea and harmonizes the whole thing.[32]

Surely one can see this give and take playing out in the Bible, such as the times when Jesus interacts playfully with individuals. He tells the woman that we don't give the children's food to dogs. She comes right back with a rejoinder, and he finally responds by crediting her with faith. Surely Jonah getting swallowed by a "big fish" then spit out on shore shows the divine playfulness and sense of humor working with creation and responding to people as they respond to and react to God.

4. Paradox
As Christian artist Michael Card sings:

For the power of paradox opens your eyes
And blinds those who say they can see
When we in our foolishness thought we were wise
He played the fool and He opened our eyes [33]

As mentioned earlier, the Bible, nature, and life are replete with paradox. Gary Hassig, in his book *Contemplation: Only the Crucified are Truly Alive*, discusses paradox. He states,

> There are also linguistic paradoxes. (*Why do we park in driveways and drive on parkways?*).... And there are natural paradoxes that reflect God's truth: Light is what makes things visible, yet light itself is invisible. The same is true with God—he opens our eyes to truth and his Kingdom, yet he can't be seen.... People try to avoid paradoxes.... [But] truly they're gateways to spiritual knowledge, which is a deeper kind of understanding that goes beyond logic.[34]

Surely we writers want to help our readers experience "gateways to spiritual knowledge" and "deeper understanding."

5. Admitting Uncertainty

The church soaked in Modernity became too obsessed with certainty, writes Peter Enns in his book, *The Sin of Certainty*. He writes of our "unexamined beliefs" and our need to let go of having to be certain (but instead, trust God ... does that sound paradoxical?).

> Accepting the challenge of an unsettled faith takes courage.... Church is too often the most dangerous place to be spiritually honest.... The secret is to de-couple our faith in God from our thoughts about God.... Faith doesn't rest in correct thinking. No one just follows the Bible. We interpret it as people with a past and present and in community with others within certain traditions. We all bring our broken and limited selves into how we think about God.[35]

Enns encourages Christians to not shy from paradox but illuminate it; to let go of fear of 'spirituality'; to learn to listen—to ourselves, to the clichés we repeat, and to others' questions, hurts, disappointments, disillusionments; to loosen up—let ourselves be playful; and to lay down our lives. "Take up your cross and let God live through us as a servant, a listener, as light, life, and love."[36]

Postmodernists have gone too far in some areas, as cultural movements tend to do. In those areas, Christians need to shine a light of truth amid relativism, order amid chaos. Elements of postmodernism that we need to resist include its rejection of universal truth or metanarrative (any over-arching story that is true for everyone). Grenz again:

> Postmodern thinkers have given up the search for universal, ultimate truth because they are convinced that there is nothing more to find than a host of conflicting interpretations or an infinity of linguistically created worlds.... In contrast to postmodern thought, we believe that there is a unifying center to reality. More specifically we acknowledge that this center has appeared in Jesus of Nazareth, who is the eternal Word present among us.... the truth of and for all humankind.[37]

In my own writing and in my publishing program through Cladach, I see the following aspects of the postmodern ethos playing out:

- Mixed-genre books that don't necessarily fit neatly into traditional bookstore categories.
- Use of "creative nonfiction" and blended writing styles, such as poetic essays.

- Openness, not dogmatism, willing to listen and dialog with other viewpoints.
- Thinking of books as adding to the conversation, deepening and moving it forward rather than expecting to have the last word.
- Making efforts to form community around authors and books (e.g., with Facebook groups, YouTube videos, and in-person events).
- Accepting that readers may find their own meaning in our writing.

Speaking to that last point, we need to realize reviewers are part of our dialog and meaning making process. If they interpret our writing differently than we meant it, we can let go of that. Yes, in a sense their interpretation is true for them. In the introduction to my first book of poetry, *Remembering Softly*, I wrote:

> I won't limit each poem's meaning by trying to explain the emotions and experiences that, for me, are encapsulated in each one. As I send them out, they are free to take on new meanings as each reader looks into them. Perhaps for you a poem will speak to a quandary, a sorrow, or a joy you are experiencing at this season of your life. That is the beauty of sharing a gift of poetry.[38]

Going further, Grenz writes about postmodernism's view of literary meanings and reader interpretation:

> Meaning is not merely a matter of what the author intended, lying in the text, waiting to be unlocked by means of scientific and empathetic interpretation. Rather, meaning emerges as the text and the interpreter engage in a dialogue.... The goal of this dialogue is

an intersection of the horizon of the author and the horizon of the interpreter.[39]

That dialog between writer and reader can break down barriers, rip open a too-tight seam of the modern crazy quilt, and identify the silvery and golden threads to weave beauty, goodness, and truth throughout the tapestry of our emerging church and world.

To conclude this chapter, I will share the advice given by William Zinsser in his classic book for writers, *On Writing Well*, speaking to writers about our use of words:

> Learn to use them with originality and care. Value them for their strength and their infinite diversity. And also remember: Somebody out there is listening.[40]

As those "Somebodies" out there listen to your writing, what will your words evoke for them?

Chapter 3

EVOKE

"[We] must also take the visible things, the things of earth, the things we think we comprehend and open them out to the heavenly, so that the familiar is for a moment transfigured and the earth, disenchanted by our dull habits, might be re-enchanted again until we see that the earth, like the heavens, is full of the glory of God."

–Malcolm Guite

"Imagination is the beginning of creation."

–George Bernard Shaw

What to publish? Controversy sells. Sex sells. Current fads sell … like a flash in the pan. Some experts tell us to write and publish to "felt needs." Others say to publish strictly within the bounds of Christian orthodoxy.

I say look to the garden again. Publish material that evokes deep wisdom, the long knowing of the mystery and meaning of life. Invoke the sacred within the mundane. Restore roots that society and church have lost, neglected, or rejected. Reach back deeply and honestly.

Learn from the garden's honeybees. The hive colony holds and communicates knowledge and wisdom gleaned by many generations of forager and worker bees. Listening to the hive's wisdom, honeybees can then fly out in a two- or three-mile radius, find the best nectar flowers, return to the hive and communicate to the others through dances that describe where and how to find the flowers, perhaps even describing the hazards as well as opportunities along the journey. In that way they are adding to, updating, and refining the hive mind.

My husband and I practiced backyard beekeeping for several years. I love watching bees on flowers. Some say flowers emit something (besides the obvious color and scent) that "calls in" the bees. Then, with so many bees giving rapt attention, even affection, to the flowers, it seems to me the plants bloom bigger and longer, sometimes much more, and longer, than they would otherwise. I have observed this phenomenon, for instance, with Peppermint flower spikes and with Blue Mist Spirea flowers. It is a "love affair," if you will. Mutual delight, certainly. With more bees in our gardens, strawberries and other fruits and vegetables grow more abundantly. In a sense, the bees remind the plants of their purpose, to bloom and produce fruit. And when flowers are pollinated, the plants produce more nectar and pollen for the bees. The bees and flowers work together.

Like bees pollinating blossoms, helping the plants remember to produce more flowers and fruit, we help readers remember their purpose and to envision possibilities in the garden of their world.

Write and publish to people whose perspectives have become narrowed and stunted, like sparse, quickly fading flowers without pollinators. Remind them who they are and what they are meant to be doing, why they are here, the joy and fulfillment of living in this created order, anticipating newness, moon rises, spring birdsong, sprouting leaves, pure pleasures that enhance, illuminate our place in the cosmos, bring responsibilities, and open potentialities.

Appealing solely to reason and offering only propositions is like standing over flowers and telling them to bloom rather than drawing them out with appeals to the depths of their creativity, goodness, and longings. "Deep calls to deep."[41] To bring people to faith and to illuminate a path forward out of deadening legalism, controlled scientism, and stale dogmatism, we need to appeal to imagination; evoke the beautiful, the good, and the true that transcend our encrusted categories, and call the listener or the reader into an experience of fresh winds, spring grasses, thawing streams, ever-new sunrises, "treasures of darkness and riches hidden in secret places," and the music of the spheres.

Poet Malcolm Guite says Jesus appeals in this way to our imagination...

> In those moments when the heavens open and the ordinary is transfigured, seen in an utterly new light.

In the gift of faith, and in Christ himself, we glimpse more than we can yet understand, our imagination apprehends more than our reason comprehends. This is not to say that the Gospel is in any way 'imaginary' in the dismissive sense of 'unreal' or 'untrue.' On the contrary it is so real and so true that we need every faculty of mind and body, including imagination, to apprehend it. In an age of linear, one-level readings of the word and the world, we need to recover confidence in the baptised imagination as a truth-bearing faculty.[42]

Therefore, don't deny imagination, but let it awaken. Create to evoke startling realizations of God's presence. Evoke the great themes of Scripture, tradition, using what C.S. Lewis called a "baptised imagination" and what others have described as "imagination redeemed." Help readers know (or remember or envision) what it truly means to be human.

Some of the best imaginative stories are consigned to children's literature shelves. I enjoyed reading the *Chronicles of Narnia* to my children and reading Andrew Peterson's *Wingfeather Saga* before giving that series to my delighted young grandsons. One could list a growing number of books that are re-enchanting Christian thinking. Surely this is a good thing. Jesus said, "unless you change and become like children, you will never enter the kingdom of heaven (Matt. 18:3)."

Imagination helped draw me into personal faith as a child and keep me there as an adult. The soil of my mind and heart was prepared by fairy stories such as those in an old book I inherited from my great grandmother, first read to me by an aunt: stories by Frances Hodgson Burnett, including "Behind the White Brick" and "The Story of Prince Fairyfoot." Later, her novel *A Secret Garden* would enchant me and then my daughter—and now a young granddaughter.

Occasionally church fed my imagination. Even as a child I loved camp meeting services in the tabernacle of Beulah Park campground nestled in the Santa Cruz Mountains of California's central coast. Outside, Redwoods and Eucalyptus trees formed naturally scented cathedrals. Inside, voices swelled and filled the huge sanctuary with melody and harmony. Music rose full-throated to the high, domed, sparkly white ceiling (that reminded me of "the Celestial City"). Adults joined in the singing with smiles or tears—sometimes both—on their faces. Often, they would lift a hand to express the words of the gospel song as their own testimony.

We didn't emphasize gifts of the Spirit much (except those of preaching, teaching, and service) in those days; but the Spirit was giving gifts of encouragement, faith, mercy. For me the greatest gifts were the sense that what was happening here was real—a reality that gave people courage and hope to go back home and live through, work through, love through the challenges of daily life and ministry.

For many of those people life was hard. Most didn't come to camp meeting to hear more expositional religious words (though those had their place). They came to be emotionally and spiritually moved, to feel closer to God and experience a touch of Heaven. The preachers I recall most vividly told stories and painted word pictures, sometimes basing an entire sermon on the creative, dramatic re-telling of a single Bible story.

My favorite camp meeting preacher was a southern orator and one-time poet laureate of his state who was known as "Poet of the Ozarks." I was writing poems even as a child, and I was enthralled that a preacher could also be a celebrated poet. And surely no one could have slept through his sermons. During one memorable sermon, adults and children sat "on the edge of the seats" as he preached on Heaven, painting a picture that filled me with wonder.

Indeed, as he exhorted in his resonate voice and gestured with his long arms, the evangelist poet began to recite an alphabetical list, in rhythmic cadence, of the things that will not be found in Heaven, from A to Z. Then, his unction lifted to a crescendo as he lilted and chanted through the alphabet again, this time exclaiming the things that *will* be in Heaven. As he described the beautiful, joyous scene, he seemed to be seeing it before his very eyes. *Amens* and *hallelujahs* from the camp meeting crowd punctuated his words.

He captured attention and kindled imaginations with his words, message, and delivery. He had obviously spent time soaking in knowledge of the Scriptures, in listening to the Spirit, and in the crafting of sentences.

Lest my readers worry, I assure you his oratory was not about God keeping out of Heaven people of certain political persuasion, color, race, gender, or religion. It was not a fear-inducing message of wrath. It was about the hope of no more pain or sickness or poverty or broken relationships or hunger or fear or oppression. He was speaking to a post-world war generation in the grips of the Cold War and worried about the "rebellious youth" of the day. These people were mostly not very powerful or prosperous. Just like any generation, they brought their experiences, training, context to the words they both spoke and heard. Their trials, fears, and needs came with them to church meetings. Savvy preachers like the poet-evangelist knew it and preached to them "where they were at."

I will add, though, that many people in that big camp meeting crowd believed anyone who wore red lipstick, drank alcoholic beverages, or went to dances or movies ... would surely not enjoy the blessings of Heaven. The rules that people hold onto for dear life will influence what they manage to hear in a spoken or written message.

A few could see beyond rules that defined holiness by

"what we don't do," to overarching themes of love calling us to compassion, joy, and freedom.

At those services and others, I became convinced—I *knew*—that there was something invisible that was even more real than the visible things around me. I'm not advocating nostalgia for the old ways. Not everything was good about the old days. But I believe we need to reach deeply into own our stories and tell them in ways that people today can hear with both mind and heart, and to which they can respond and build on in the present and into the future.

At campmeeting the kids gathered afternoons with a wonderful child-evangelist couple. One year that enthusiastic man and wife enthrallingly presented the story of *Pilgrim's Progress* using a dramatic script and colorful, beautiful flannelgraph scenes. We kids came eagerly each day for the next installment of the story.

When the movie *Noah* (with Russel Crowe) came out, it was met with scorn by evangelicals who had propositionally believed that the Sunday school tellings of Noah and the Ark were the whole, entire, literal story. The movie didn't look like the flannelgraph presentations of their childhood or the bare-bones account in the Bible. The film *Noah* was broadly condemned by evangelicals for its too creative re-telling. (Turns out it was told more through a lens of Jewish tradition.) I admit a few aspects of Darren Aronofsky's film were somewhat unsettling (not always a bad thing to be unsettled); but I liked it, especially two mental pictures it left with me. First was the scene with Methuselah (the oldest man who ever lived and Noah's grandfather) busy searching for a rare, ripe berry to eat as the waters rose closer and closer. He wisely saw, with long vision, that water meant hope. He had long soaked in the beauty, goodness, and re-creative power of the earth and the Creator. He had no doubt long prayed for renewal on the earth. He didn't fear the flood.

Second, toward the end of the film, in a touching scene of reconciliation, as the character Noah came to terms with the trauma of witnessing all those deaths, and as he suffered survivor's guilt, he and his wife were kneeling on the ground. Even as all the horror, hard work, doubts showed in their creased faces, they sifted their fingers through refreshed soil—choosing to believe in beauty, goodness, newness. This was surely another picture of hope.

In the movie script, Noah had come to the realization that when he freely chose love and mercy, he had done what God had hoped he would do, what God had wanted him to do. As I watched the Noah character and his wife together with all their pain and trauma and weariness, face to face on living earth, fingering the living soil, removing a few small rocks, I was reminded that life gives us the gift of creativity, seeds of renewal and resurrection. To work soil is, at least in part, to remember from whence we come, to keep our roots alive and let them nourish us; but to choose to look with hope toward, and work for, a future.

Today we are easily flooded with impatience, animosity, violence, ugliness, compartmentalization, nihilism, and isolation. Or maybe these things make us ripe for a flood of some kind. We can soak in virtual reality, choose-your-own-identity and avatar type non-living. But I remind myself: "The Light has come, and the darkness cannot put it out." Grace, hope, light, love abide in the very fabric, the very soil of life. Creation contains the ability to heal. Jesus' resurrection assures us God knows how to break into and out of dark places, bringing life out of death. Jesus always has and always will keep showing up. As Gerard Manley Hopkins expressed it, "Christ plays in ten-thousand places."

Writers can use creative imagination to evoke visions of the unseen, open cracks for the light to shine into this present grayness. Soak in the Light and evoke the Light for readers.

We confess belief in God's omnipresence. Yet we constantly pray "Be with So-n-So" and "God, come down." Truly it did feel like the glory "fell" in some revival services I experienced as a child. When I gaze at a dazzling sunset, the glory is "out there." We come to feel that God is out there, too: somewhere beyond, absent from us, watching from above, keeping score. But some theologians, and certainly Scripture does, teach that God is constantly working *in* us, relating *to* us, calling us to walk *in* and *partner with* the divine. We can pray that the eyes of our hearts will open to see God, that our hearts will welcome, respond to, and cooperate with God who is *here, now*. Our part as writers and publishers is to use words to evoke for others this presence, this wooing, this call and response, this life of the sacred in the mundane.

Perhaps we not only paint pictures with our words but also create contexts in which God can work. In our post-Christian, technology-focused, personally-isolated world of increasing instability, as familiar structures and institutions crumble, can we heed words such as those written by N.T. Wright during the Covid-19 Pandemic? He wrote that it may be

> …time to lament and be active participants with God in holding sorrow before the Father … creating a context for multiple works of healing and hope.[43]

How do we, through our words, "create context"? As I discussed in Chapter 1, the writer's and the publisher's first work is to soak in and soak up God's presence, then give to others out of the overflow of love, joy, and peace. Then create something beautiful. As a beautiful gothic cathedral, a symphony concert, or simply a garden path provides context for experiencing and opening oneself to the presence of God, so a narrative in story or essay or poem or book form may provide a context that evokes and invokes and invites sacred encounters between the reader and God.

In *Ekstasis Magazine*, Paul Anleitner has written,

> Consider the moment a call to recover our Christian vocation, to reject the incessant culture war which only serves to scar the world, obscuring the view of the beautiful from the hungry eyes that long to see her. Instead let us plant vineyards in Babylon and grow something beautiful [in exile].[44]

In Fyodor Dostoevsky's novel *The Idiot*, Prince Myshkin, the protagonist famously says, "I believe the world will be saved by beauty." I think I believe that also, more and more.

Contemporary Canadian philosopher Charles Taylor, in his book *A Secular Age*, argues that our modern, buffered selves are isolated from a sense of the transcendent. "Buffer" brings to my mind a fabric protector that prevents spills from soaking into a tablecloth, upholstered furniture, or carpet.

Modernity has surrounded the self with a protective coating or buffer zone. For instance, much of our communications and experience is buffered through technology. Furthermore, often we live as though all that exists are the things we can study, measure, and control. Robert Barron (and others) say this is doing damage to the human spirit. When Barron speaks or writes on this subject, he declares,

> I say punch holes in the buffered self and open yourself to transcendence.... [Many today have] soaked too long in the acids of ... skepticism and materialism and lived too long in the musty confines of the buffered self.[45]

Leonard Cohen's famous lyrics offer a poetic version of this thought:

Ring the bells that still can ring
Forget your perfect offering
There is a crack in everything
That's how the light gets in[46]

Harking back to the gardening analogy, perhaps the modern, buffered self is like the rocky ground where the sown seeds can't take root and the buried seeds can't sprout. Let's begin to break up the fallow ground, to remove rocks, to aerate or poke holes in the buffering crust and smothering thatch. It may take time and patience. This process will likely not be completed in my lifetime or the lifetime of the books I write and/or publish; but I and they can be part of the process and the work God is desiring to do through and with us and others who follow us.

Let us envision holes punched in the impacted, hard, buffering soil of modern minds and hearts, encouraging and restoring healthy organisms in the soil, pollinators on blossoms, insects helping to maintain natural balance. Like bees reminding plants to bloom, our words can invoke, remind, and add true, beautiful, health-giving thoughts, images, and narratives that open cracks and help the light get through encrusted minds.

Philip Yancey, in his memoir, *Where the Light Fell*, quotes Saint Augustine: "I couldn't look at the sun directly, but I could look at where the light fell." Yancey said for a time he couldn't look directly at God because he had been scorched by his received image of God as a bully.

> Then I realized whoever was responsible for this world was an artist.... Nature, classical music, and romantic love is where the light fell for me.... [Often] the church has not been a healing force but a divisive force.[47]

I hope our books—those of faith-based writers and publishers—will be a healing force. I hope we can evoke with our words places where the light can fall for those who are blinded by the buffer zones of modern and postmodern life (and, may I add, by bad theology as well as bad representation of God by many Christian leaders and fellow believers).

As author and musician Andrew Peterson says,

> Somewhere out there, men and women with redeemed, integrated imaginations are sitting down to spin a tale that awakens, a tale that leaves the reader with a painful longing that points them home, a tale whose fictional beauty begets beauty in the present world and heralds the world to come. Someone out there is building a bridge so we can slip across to elf-land and smuggle back some of its light into this present darkness.[48]

I hear echoes of what C.S. Lewis experienced when his imagination awakened—in reading, as a young atheist, George MacDonald's *Phantastes*.

These days faith-based publishing involves a long vision yet is immediate, personal, and specific. We must be patient but grounded to reinvigorate the soil and rebuild the ecosystem. Some Christian writers, thinkers, theologians say God's providence is dependent on the integrity of ecosystems. This makes sense to me and I think it fits with scripture.

We may need to recognize the bleakness of our situation before we can realize how glad are the tidings of Jesus. But we must then pay the price of giving up gloominess and make a "sacrifice of praise." Then we can work with writing to evoke a sense of home that brings awareness to readers of their lostness and longings. Evoke a sense of the Garden, of harmony, meaning, wholeness, of desperate hope in the midst of battle, the power of perseverance and compassion.

A writer can invoke a mood, feeling, spirit using words that employ metaphor, analogy, and symbol. A writer can evoke a scene, an imaginary world, a character's personality. But the reader needs some experience or awareness or vocabulary with which to imagine ("see," "hear," "smell," "taste," and "feel") it for themselves. They need at least some experience or memory to compare and/or contrast with the thing, concept, or scene being described. In a sense we can't bring forth something new with our written words without first reaching into our past and the readers' pasts.

I see this principle in the conversations of Sam and Frodo as they near Mordor toward the end of Peter Jackson's film version of *The Return of the King*. As the two hobbits labor through heavier and heavier trials to enter Mordor, they finally lie exhausted in the dark. Sam crawls over to Frodo, holds him in his arms, and asks,

> 'Do you remember the Shire, Mr. Frodo? It'll be spring soon, and the orchards will be in blossom; and the birds will be nesting in the hazel thicket; and they'll be sowing the summer barley in the

lower fields; and eating the first of the strawberries with cream.... Do you remember the taste of strawberries?' Frodo shuts his eyes and whispers weakly, 'No, Sam. I can't recall ... the taste of food; nor the sound of water; nor the touch of grass.'[49]

The oppressive, controlling shadow of Mordor had dimmed his memory, dulled his senses, and darkened his vision. Then, after the ring sinks into the burning lava of Mordor, in the cataclysmic landscape erupting and exploding all around, the Hobbits stagger and run till they find a rock to rest upon and wait for what they think is "the end of all things." Frodo, now free from the power and control of the ring, begins to remember again. In awe he says,

'I can see the Shire ... the Brandywine River, Bag End, Gandalf's fireworks ... the lights in the Party Tree.'[50]

Technology gives us power. We come to love it as "precious" for that reason. We cannot imagine life without it. We gaze at it as often as we can. It somehow makes us "more" than we are. We feel magnified. And we can choose to be invisible, anonymous, even as we can possibly "reach" so many connections "out there."

But we are in danger of diminishing in spirit, in our sense of the realness of the real, losing connection to what is embodied, incarnate, and grounding.

In the eighth chapter of Luke, Jesus heals a girl pronounced dead. He tells the grieving family and friends, "Do not fear. Only believe, and she will be saved.... She is not dead but sleeping." When he took her hand and told her to rise, we are told "Her spirit returned, and she got up."

In Jesus' parable of the Prodigal Son (Luke 15), after the prodigal had wasted his fortune and was reduced to feeding pigs, according to verse 17, he "came to himself."

Surely we all know people who seem spiritually dispirited, lost, even dead. Perhaps we can write and publish narratives to help their "spirits return," to help them "wake up" and "come to themselves."

In my childhood, I remember waking up mornings to the sounds of birds singing, wind blowing, rain drops falling, crickets chirping, my father whistling, my mother singing, planes flying over, the cat purring, bacon sizzling, the coffee pot percolating. How is thought and perception different for kids who grow up hearing the constant droning and blaring of the television, or now with constant, ear-bud-mediated sounds, or Siri's voice giving reports, questions, answers, and directions? (These things can and do add to our lives; but we need to make space for nature and all the senses. Even in urban settings a person can keep houseplants and small pets, sing songs, play guitar, and bake chocolate chip cookies.)

Speaking and writing starts with listening, hearing, touching, thinking, intuiting, patiently waiting for something fresh to say. Technology is a boon in many ways, but we need to undertake times of fasting from visual media. Allow space for imagination. Get into nature, into the wilds, into a garden. In *Adorning the Dark*, Andrew Peterson speaks of the importance of having a discipline or practice in your life that doesn't involve a computer screen; that gets you outside in creation, in which you get your hands dirty. This practice, such as hiking or gardening, will connect you with others, with your own heart, and with "realities greater than yourself," reminding you that "the world is real and it is brimming with God's presence. This can only help your writing."[51]

When Carol O'Casey queried me about publishing her book, *Unwrapping Wonder*, she wrote:

> Heeding technology's cry to get connected can result in overloaded circuits of the mind. Frenetic connections can cause frazzled lives. *Unwrapping Wonder: Finding Hope in the Gift of Nature* will restore the reader's soul as they step outside to cultivate a connection with creation and deepen their relationship with the Creator. *Unwrapping Wonder* is a delightful mix of natural history, human story and God's glory found in everyday nature. Based on Job's words in 12:7—'But ask the animals, and they will teach you, or the birds of the air, and they will tell you, or let the fish of the sea inform you'—each chapter will focus on one ordinary natural object, such as the bee, the barnacle, the tiniest seed.[52]

Carol captured my interest! I published the book.

Another famous line from Gerard Manley Hopkins is "The world is charged with the grandeur of God." Similarly, Flannery O'Connor spoke of the South (where she lived and of which she wrote in her novels and short stories) as being "Christ-haunted." I believe in a sense the whole world is Christ-haunted and we must let ourselves feel that hauntedness until we can embed it—each in our own style—within the words and stories we write and publish.

The world is broken, and evil exercises influence. But light shines in the darkness. There's nothing truly beautiful, such as music, art, and poetry, that doesn't point us toward God.

According to Charles Taylor there has been a shift in Western thought and consciousness from hundreds of years ago when the question, "Do you believe in God" was considered a viable question. That was before modernism bifurcated the sacred and the secular. The transcendent shrank and the imminent expanded. But today people are again becoming interested in the possibilities of the transcendent. We writers and publishers are given a challenge and opportunity to be agents of renewal in the world. We can let the discussions like the one in this chapter help form our goals of what to write and publish.

This vision and process I'm trying to explore with you, requires both courage and humility. As Madeleine L'Engle wrote in *Walking on Water*,

> We have to be braver than we think we can be, because God is constantly calling us to be more than we are, to see through plastic sham to living, breathing reality, and to break down our defenses of self-protection in order to be free to receive and give love.[53]

L'Engle explains that the words for human and humility come from the same root, *humus* (earth). In Jesus' parable of the seed and the sower, the farmer/gardener must trust that he is not wasting the seed, that rain will fall, that sun will shine and warm, that at least some of the seed will fall on ready soil. The farmer is a co-creator with God; and, as writers and publishers, so are we.

We used to sing songs about "glory" out there somewhere beyond the clouds, where God was, perhaps on a heavenly throne. Now I am thinking of the transcendent glory that is imminently present in and with us—with all of us as creatures, in the inter-connectedness and the beauty of nature, of babies, of dying saints, of seasonal changes, of plays of light and shapes, colors, textures all around us, of moments of awareness that awaken us, even if briefly, to something more than the mechanistic, and measurable;

something closer than our breath; but something of which we only receive glimpses.

> He is the image of the invisible God ... all things have been created through him and for him ... and in him all things hold together (Col. 1:15-17).

Immediate things that "take us up" into the experience of the transcendent include poetry, worship, nature, music, art, friendship. These are aided by intuition, synchronicity, contemplation, meditation, dreams, and rituals that bring a sense of togetherness and connectedness in and across time and space.

Readers today have plenty of books offering rational explanations and reasoned arguments for why and how to follow Christ. I am writing this at the beginning of the Advent season. I will close this chapter with a poem by Madeleine L'Engle and the perspective it evokes, as well as the new thing it provokes:

After Annunciation

*This is the irrational season
when love blooms bright and wild.
Had Mary been filled with reason
there'd have been no room for the child.*[54]

Chapter 4

PROVOKE

"And let us consider how to provoke one another to love and good deeds..."

—Hebrews 10:24

"It is time to be ... deft and strategic, subversive, surprising, amusing, able to offer the occasional 'shock of recognition' that reminds and reawakens."

—Marilyn McEntyre

"The best books do the unexpected. As we read them, they read us. And though the book stays the same, we leave the pages forever changed."

—Allen Arnold

We writers provoke with words, phrases, sentences, paragraphs, stories, essays, ideas, themes, observations, and imagery. But if we are provocative simply for the sake of being hip and inciting reactions, where is the good in that? Likewise, what good is accomplished by inducing guilt or despair or pining for the past? Provoking must prod toward life and orient toward the future. Surely, we want our words to kindle clear thinking, renewed perspectives, commitment to healthy relationships, and genuinely, generatively loving actions.

Write and publish to rouse the dozing and the dazed to waken to visions of what could be. "Without a vision the people perish" (Prov. 29:18). Our readers need something to buoy them in the sufferings of life, something to help them sustain meaning, purpose, and hope.

In gardens we wait, anticipate, plan, and prepare—always with an orientation to the future. Even in times of dormancy, even when "prophesying over dry bones (Ez. 37:4)" or "breaking up fallow ground (Hos. 10:12)," we call and inspire readers to be renewed, have courage, take action, join hands, bear fruit, give thanks.

With our words we may choose to provoke anger or love, fear or courage, bitterness or release. Sometimes our words use irony to stimulate discussion in order to reach a new understanding. Jesus did this. For instance, in answering the Syrophoenician woman (Mk. 7:24-30), his words provoked her to argue with him. Then, rather than being put off, Jesus praised the woman for her faith.

We can't control listeners' or readers' reactions. Far better than words and texts that just tickle the fancy, scratch an itch, or whitewash the surface, we are after transformation, and that may seem to hurt before it helps. Does it irk you when readers and reviewers misunderstand, apply their own contexts and prejudices to your words? Know and remember that God is with others as well as with you; look for God in everyone and everything.

Try to meet "felt needs" and address current issues. But also seek to understand the deeper needs of the day.

Writers and publishers are—or should be—thought leaders. You can sharpen your own thinking as well as that of your readers by stirring up conversation. Bring together different "sides" to talk with each other. Provoke response, feelings, questions. Remember to gently "poke holes in the buffered self" (as discussed in the previous chapter). Perhaps in that way we can help create a future for humankind and God's kingdom come. As Marilyn McEntyre states,

> Life-giving conversations require a willingness to wake up, be aware, peer into the darkness, consider and consult and open our imaginations to perilous possibilities. Because it is in that darkness that the Light shines—there where the Word, which was in the beginning, emerges from the deeps of cosmic silence and summons us to listen and learn so that we may hear the word given to each of us to embody and speak into the world while we are here.[55]

This prompts me to ask, "Are we embodying and speaking" consistently into the world? In older parlance, does our walk match our talk? Wouldn't God's kingdom come more fully through us and among us, and God's shalom flourish more in this world, if we Christians' beliefs matched our actions—if we quit expending our energies defending worn-out dogmas and doctrines that aren't helping people, and may even be hindering free questions of growth and faith? I agree with scientist, minister, and author Tim Reddish:

> At the end of the day, a theology that is not also grounded in reality, our experience, will not be taken seriously—either by ourselves or by others.[56]

This process of "getting real" about what we believe so we can live it out, will transform our writing and publishing into co-laboring and co-creating with Creator God who is present and active in our world, in the church, and with each of us. Theologian and author Thomas Jay Oord declares:

> Created creatures co-create with their Creator.... God acts to empower, inspire, and lure others in each moment.... God may suggest ideas, call for actions, nudge toward possibilities, entice toward beauty, convince it's time to tear down for a rebuild, and more.[57]

I want to co-create with God in such a way that the Great Poet can use the books I publish to (in Oord's provocative words) empower, inspire, entice, convince, nudge, suggest, and call. As potential life is "in" the seed and seed is planted "in" the soil, so the resulting fruit will be "in" those who eat it. When you read an absorbing book or delightful poem, the phrases, the images, the characters, the perspectives, the insights become part of you.

I like to think that God is present to me and my author friends as we write, edit, publish, and market books! To think that God—whose essence can be described as unchanging love—is at the same time truly and experientially with us, even in our writing and publishing work. God can also be in the seeds (essays, books, blog posts, poems) we sow. To think that those who eat the fruit of the seeds, who read and digest the words and are in some way nourished, sustained, and changed by them ... are in this process potentially experiencing and relating to the Creator themselves!

Some religious thinkers describe God as the great Artist or Poet of the world. Often, in a mystical but real way, I feel help comes, guides my thinking, makes suggestions, gives mental pictures. My grandfather, a preacher who wrote verse, said (with a grin) that sometimes a muse sat on his shoulder. This intuition makes sense to wordsmiths who marvel when inspiration appears and provokes them to write. Poets and writers who want to evoke and provoke will search, listen, wait, and watch for best expressions, forms, images and words. As Mark Twain is quoted as saying, "To get the right word in the right place is a rare achievement." Often one senses they are not alone in the process.

This creature-Creator creating is not prescriptive but open ended, letting breezes blow in. Theologian Catherine Keller, herself a wordsmith extraordinaire, exclaims:

> Scripture is littered with broken words, words breaking open new meanings, breaking open closed systems. The Bible brims with metaphor, trope, figure of speech, parable, psalm, prayer, story. When abstract propositions of belief that are rare in scripture become fixed in a closed system, the fallacious factualism kicks in. The propositions then draw our concern away from the concrete processes of our shared creaturely life, rather than spiritually illumining them.[58]

Biblical truth and the experience of relationship with God and each other in this world cannot be fully and livingly described as facts, lists of dos and don'ts, or doctrinal statements even. I don't want to write, publish, read, or internalize what Keller describes as "fallacious factualism" and "propositions," but stories, poetry, narrative, a vision shared in heart language of "shared creaturely life."

As Robert Barron comments, adding to this conversation from another angle:

> I have believed for some time that this issue of *how* we communicate is perhaps as important as *what* we communicate—that is, if we are interested in moving [provoking?] the conversation beyond a very narrow circle.[59]

Authors who have widened and spiritually illuminated my horizons with how as well as what they write include George MacDonald, Madeleine L'Engle, Leif Enger, River Jordan, Wendell Berry, and many sensitive, bold, thoughtful and creative others.

If, then, relational and provocative narrative is the means, what is the message? What seeds are needed? What crops/plants will grow in this season? If you believe in the centrality of the Incarnation, as I do, then we believe Jesus brought Light and Life into a darkened world and showed us, by his words and actions, how to do the same. According to scripture, the pre-incarnate Christ has been present in, to, and through creation from the beginning.

> All things came into being through him.... What has come into being in him was life, and the life was the light of all people, and without him not one thing came into being.... (John 1:3-4)

The process of things coming into being require cooperation and response. Like wordsmiths casting about, seeking for the right word, so God the Artist searches, waits, calls forth newness and willing participation. The incarnation story came together when the time and place and people came together and said yes to the perfect expression of God's essence of Love and perfect embodiment of God's Presence. Mary said yes to the invitation to carry—and give birth to—the son of God. Brad Jersak comments,

> ...God's reign of love in the world always involves willing participants. But this process also always starts with an invitation by God's Spirit to engage in plans he has been orchestrating well in advance.... Mary's example challenges us to likewise say our willing 'yes' to partnership with God.[60]

Incarnation gave us Jesus and a picture of God that we can embrace, emulate, and relate to in such a way as to experience everlasting, fruitful, creative life. When we are in Christ and Christ is in us, we want to share this experience with the world. In writing about the parable of the sower, Robert Barron adds,

> Keep in mind that Jesus himself in person is the seed sown. Jesus is the seed that wants to take root in us. This seed is sown far and wide, through all sorts of means. It is destined for the whole world.[61]

To sow life-giving seeds of true, artistic expression and helpful, life-giving, Christ-carrying words through publishing in today's world, we need to offer a vision not just for being transformed individually but also for transforming our communities, societies, and ecosystems. Forgiveness, reconciliation, freedom; and the fellowship and healing of loving community are needed.

Famous newspaper publisher Joseph Pulitzer is said to have embraced this motto: "Comfort the afflicted and afflict the comfortable." Do you think this is a good motto for a provocative Christian writer and publisher?

Jesus gave comfort to the afflicted. He saw the real needs of individuals and responded in compassion and healing. Today, God works through people to lift up those who are burdened, oppressed, and bereft; to build them up in love and faith to sustain them in the difficulties of life.

On the other hand, Jesus often unsettles us—afflicts us, if you will—with his words and actions. He criticized the religious and political establishments. He gave his time and attention to the weak, the sick, the unlovely, the estranged, rejected and powerless. He spoke directly to the heart.

We writers are uniquely positioned to challenge and unsettle those who are insulated in ease. And perhaps we need to remind ourselves of Jesus' call to feed the hungry, bind up wounds, and comfort those who mourn.

To be used this way, we may need to move out of our shallow thinking and playing it safe. Read Jesus' Sermon on the Mount. Read the Acts of the Apostles. Read about the lives and deaths of Christian saints, mystics, and martyrs.

I have published books that might afflict readers out of false comfort and into a life of more compassion and faith. For instance:

1. Judith Pex's memoir of their work in Eilat, Israel, describes her and John's thirty years of friendship ministry and service in Israel. The accounts in *Come Stay Celebrate* can fortify the reader with the desire to live out the life of Jesus, perhaps even opening their home, their arms, or time, and give themselves to reach others around them—including many outcasts—with God's love.

2. Stories in Pex's *A People Tall and Smooth* of Christian (and one Muslim) refugees fleeing the

genocide in South Sudan will disturb readers' ease but may also give perspective on the troubles traumatized refugees face.

3. Reading *Hostage In Taipei* about the Alexander family's hostage experience at the hands of a Taiwanese terrorist may afflict the reader with a realization of what potential for evil exists in the world and the unsettling question of "What would I do? How would I react?"; or the Alexander's story may give comfort to see how the Alexanders showed love and shared hope with the very man who caused them great bodily injury and emotional harm.

4. Janyne McConnaughey's *Brave* series of memoirs about how she accepted her need for healing when she was 61 years of age and a long-time successful college professor. She admits and shares how her inner life was falling apart and she entered years of therapy, working hard to integrate her many "selves." Fascinating reading and surely both afflicting to those Christians who can't or don't want to admit their need, and comforting to those who feel their need but also feel all alone in their pain and don't know where to start and how to have hope for healing.

Open your hearts to what our Lord, Jesus Christ, who himself comforted the afflicted and afflicted the comfortable, may be saying to you. Do you write and publish books that mainly offer escape or make readers feel good about their chosenness and security or feel justified in excluding others because "evil doers are going to hell and getting what they deserve"? Are you helping readers feel even more comfortable with the familiar?

I hope not. Our books need to challenge, maybe even afflict with a desire to show compassion to the marginalized, risk stepping out of familiar zones, and open to the new things God is (always) doing.

The first book I published through Cladach was the story of a Cambodian Buddhist/Animist boy in a jungle village whose seeming-idyllic life was destroyed by the Khmer Rouge. He suffered first-hand the unspeakable horror of Pol Pot's Killing Fields, met (and was met by) Jesus in a refugee camp, later became a Christian pastor in California ... and my friend.

That book, *No More Fear: From Killing Fields to Harvest Fields*, was published twenty-five years ago, in the lengthy aftermath of the Vietnam era, the Cold War, rampant inflation, then injustices in corporate takeovers and restructurings, as well as turmoil in the Middle East. In those days, we Christians were still rather certain about our propositional statements of belief, and transactional in our presentations of the gospel.

These days, drastic change continues, after 9/11, continuing Middle East wars, worldwide refugee crises, deepening divides in society. We are seeing the proliferation and increasing power and influence of (and anxiety related to) the Internet, social media, AI (artificial intelligence), pandemics, climate instability, environmental disasters, and new threats of nuclear war. Leaders at every level and in every place in this shrinking world (both time and space seem to be compacting) are flailing about for how to make decisions and how to best lead. Not a pretty picture. Where is beauty in the world, let alone goodness and truth?

Has the world become too ugly to love or redeem? No, says minister and author Patricia Adams Farmer, not when we have such a beautiful God:

Beauty seems to be lost! But we know differently. Beauty cannot be drowned. It cannot be swept away. It will not give up or give in. And in the ruins of tragedy, God never stops luring, creating, transforming, redeeming, and loving things back into life and wholeness.[62]

Has the world changed so much that Christians can no longer effectively speak into it? No; not if we resist the urge to dogmatically proclaim the imminent intervention and judgment of a wrathful God. Instead, we must speak/write the truth of God's life-giving presence with the experience of God's love in our attuned hearts and lives, and with God's intimate presence and poetic creativity in our spoken and printed words.

Publishing, like life itself, like beauty shining vulnerably into an oft-hostile world, involves risk (e.g., *Will readers reject this book? Will an author engage in the promotional and relational process? Are we wasting time, energy, and resources?*). Surely God is not calling us to a life of safety and security. In the words of theologian Thomas Jay Oord again,

> Mission is risky business. It means taking chances and being susceptible to failure. But God seems the biggest risk taker of all! Mission requires vulnerability. It involves a measure of dependence upon those not always dependable. Convincing others—through our lives, our relationships, and our ideas—means risking rejection. Mission requires humility.... Humility is risky. And yet God took the ultimate risk in the self-giving love of Jesus.[63]

Why should we care about such a Christ-resistant world and set-in-its-ways church? Because God cares. Because God calls us to mission. I think we can invest self-givingly in such a way that we begin to see the intrinsic goodness of the world. This is a timely and critical point for Christians today. We need to open our unbuffered eyes to the beauty around us. I think many Christians have put on blinders, have so long thought of "the world" as so dark, doomed, and depraved that they cannot recognize the divine presence that is enlivening all things. Consequently their "truth" has shriveled into pills to swallow, like taking vegetable capsules and forgoing real, earthy, hearty vegetables that are nurtured by soil and sun and rain.

In *Love and the Postmodern Predicament* Christian philosopher D.C. Schindler makes a case, as I understand it, that transcendentals (as properties of being) are immanent in all things in a way that calls us to them and reveals reality so we can then respond in right relationship to God, others, and creation. He states,

> A radically good world calls us out of ourselves and into itself by its very nature, and thus our interaction involves our very selves in response.[64]

God has come into the world, responding to it with God's very self. Jesus' feet got dirty walking dusty paths. I say let's get our feet and hands dirty, digging in the soil and planting seeds of Christ by speaking, writing, working to increase health, well-being, and beauty in our world, encouraging people to see *what is*, all around them.

My father, as a boy, had to work the fields of his father's farm in western Kansas. It was late Dust Bowl era. Daddy said they could tell which way the wind was blowing by the color of the dust in the air. If it was black, it was blowing down from the Black Hills of South Dakota. If red, it was blowing up from Oklahoma's Red River. When the nearly destitute young family first arrived at the farm, they found the topsoil blown in piles against the fences. They labored to eke out a living. When rain came, it often fell too hard and didn't soak in, but just ran off the crusted soil.

Much later, after thirty years of laboring in the field of church pastorates in California and Oregon, Daddy lost his sweetheart and ministry partner when my mother died at age 48. During their last pastorate together, he had taken up organic gardening. At the same time, the main theme of his message became love. The district superintendent, his friend, had sent him to "save" a small church being disrupted by various influences and to bring it into line with denominational standards and doctrine. But Daddy instead found himself simply loving the people in that beautiful river valley in eastern Oregon. My parents invested themselves fully in nurturing relationships, speaking wisdom into confused thinking, and working to heal brokenness. He likened it to what he was learning about organic gardening, in which one works to improve the health of the soil first, rather than just applying chemical insecticides and artificial fertilizers to stimulate quick but unsustainable growth and bloom. I was especially impressed with his huge, steaming compost pile and loamy soil. In those days he wrote a little poem that contained the lines:

> *The soft gentle mist soaks*
> *finally better than the deluge.*

Then Mother got cancer. The church people prayed and prayed. She miraculously recovered. I wrote a piece about this miracle, that was accepted by our denominational magazine. But by the time the publication came out, cancer had shown up in many parts of her body and in a short time it took her life. Daddy eventually returned to seminary to earn higher degrees and start a second career as a licensed counselor.

Later, after retiring from counseling, my dad's third career was writing, and I helped him publish his book on marriage. On the last walk I took with him, when he was ninety, we spoke of Heaven and how little we know about it.

He expressed his belief that the tree, fruit, and leaves described in Revelation symbolize the work waiting for those in the afterlife. Perhaps those who have embraced self-giving love will continue to participate in the healing of the world:

> Then the angel showed me the river of the water of life, bright as crystal, flowing from the throne of God and of the Lamb through the middle of the street of the city. On either side of the river, is the tree of life with its twelve kinds of fruit, producing its fruit every month; and the leaves of the tree are for the healing of the nations (Rev. 22:1-2).

Perhaps even now Daddy is consuming the healing fruit, or whatever that activity symbolizes, in some mysterious way still able to join God in loving the world into a better existence.

I want to do what I can through the ministry of writing and publishing to improve the soil, sow good seed, and share the gentle, soaking rain of God's love. God's work in this world is a process we can participate in. Process thinker Jay McDaniel gives some guidance to my publishing goals when he writes that this way of thinking will

> ...build upon the past, point toward the future, care for the Earth, care for people, and add beauty to the world ... a way of living in the world that embodies respect and care for the community of life.[65]

In the 1970s and 80s, in my youth, some of us embraced a back-to-nature way of life, with natural foods, organic gardening, creating things by hand, and sharing life in a more tangible, personal way than we often do today. At that time, many of us were touched by the Charismatic Movement, seeking a more immediate, relational and experiential expression of faith and Christian community. Singing "Kumbaya," holding hands in a prayer circle, experiencing miracles, feeling the love ... was renewing; but some of the excitement didn't last. Soon the need for solid beliefs became evident. When I questioned a friend about the misuse of scripture, I received the answer, "We don't need theology. We just need the Holy Spirit!"

We wanted to experience Jesus' love. But Kumbaya expressions of faith, and preoccupation with Jesus' soon return, wasn't a solid enough foundation when tragedies, evils, and brokenness came into the lives of people and of churches. When we realized we weren't being rescued out of this world's overwhelming challenges and sufferings, we had to find a way to live in it faithfully and fruitfully. Years later I read these words by German theologian Jürgen Moltmann:

> The coming lordship of the risen Christ cannot be merely hoped for and awaited. This hope and expectation also sets its stamp on life, action and suffering in the history of society. Hence mission means not mere propagation of faith and hope, but also historic transformation of life.... Not to be conformed to this world does not mean merely to be transformed in oneself, but to transform in opposition and creative expectation the face of the world, in the midst of which one believes, hopes and loves. The hope of the gospel has a polemic and liberating relation not only to the religions and ideologies of men, but still more to the factual, practical life of men and to the relationships in which this life is lived.[66]

If we don't have our minds and hearts too much on past glories or on a vague hope of escapist heavenly glories, we can still make a difference by embracing what God is active in, and calling us to participate in now. For as another wise author, Franciscan contemplative Richard Rohr has written,

> Transformation more often happens not when something new begins but when something old falls apart. The pain of something old falling apart—chaos—invites the soul to listen at a deeper level. It invites … the soul to go to a new place because the old place is falling apart.[67]

Many things seem to be falling apart in the world and the church. I find myself beginning to, in Rohr's words, "listen at deeper levels" and my "soul going to new places." It's still as true as it was in the 60s and 70s, as the popular song said, "What the world needs now is love, sweet love / It's the only thing that there's just too little of." I hope we can let the love we sing about, only with better, renewed understanding of what Tom Oord calls "self-giving, others-empowering love," re-invigorate our lives, relationships, communities, and our systems of belief. I hope to do my small part.

Throughout human history God has been drawing "all people" to himself, using the means at hand. Though the soil may seem unresponsive, rocky, unbalanced, and malnourished these days, we can partner with God in breaking up the fallow ground and regenerating the soil (see Hos. 10:12) hands-on, here-and-now.

Writers and publishers can be hindered by perfectionism and pride. We must let go of the desire to communicate the last word, the final word, the complete story, the whole truth. Rather, we need to communicate something real to life, relevant within context, and true to revelation and experience. A preacher or writer won't have the whole, final answer no matter how hard they try. Anyway, more effective is to realize we are adding to the conversation. Prompt discussion and dialog. Pique curiosity and thought. Provoke people to search, seek, wrestle, and question.

The post-postmodern (or metamodern) word *Ironesty* applies here (defined as being sincere though not cringe-worthy while acknowledging—and not shying away from—irony). For, as Thomas Merton wrote,

> Sincerity is, perhaps, the most vitally important quality of true prayer [and prayer may be the true ground of effective writing]. It [sincerity] is the only valid test of our faith, our hope, and our love of God. No matter how deep our meditations ... how noble our thought about the mysteries of God; they are all useless if we do not really mean what we say.[68]

Merton then quotes Jesus quoting the prophet Isaiah:

> 'You hypocrites! Isaiah prophesied rightly about you when he said: "This people honors me with their lips, but their hearts are far from me"' (Matt. 15:7-8).

Jesus was provocative there, as Isaiah had been before him. They spoke with authenticity and honesty, and with a certain irony. Later, when the resurrected Christ appeared first in a garden, mistaken as the gardener, one finds both irony and sincerity, as pointed out by Barron:

> In paradise (the word itself denotes 'walled garden'), our first parents were secure and innocent, but in the manner of inexperienced children. Leaving paradise was, in one sense, a positive move, for it permitted them to grow up, to engage the chaos of the unknown creatively and intelligently. This reading of Genesis,

which has roots in Tillich, Hegel, and others, permits us to see that the goal of the spiritual life is not a simple return to the garden of dreaming innocence, but rather an inhabiting of the garden on the far side of the cross, that place where the tomb of Jesus was situated and in which the risen Christ appeared precisely as 'gardener.'[69]

Jesus allowing Mary to think he was a gardener as she grieved with downcast vision in the garden, was powerfully pointing to a truth and a potential for which she and his other followers were not yet ready. To get from the one garden to the other, the disciples of Jesus needed to experience Pentecost—to be stoked with the fire of the Holy Spirit.

Sometimes farmers will burn an entire field to destroy invasive weeds and organisms. Then they will regenerate and renew the soil to start afresh. If we try to write and publish to provoke—in our own power—we will accomplish little for God's kingdom. If we listen to and work *with* God, our writing will provoke for renewal. Meanwhile, we daily have our small fires to keep stoked, as we shall see in the next chapter.

Chapter 5

STOKE

"Since, then, we have such a hope, we act with great boldness."

–2 Cor. 3:12

"And this, our life, exempt from public haunt, finds tongues in trees, books in the running brooks, sermons in stones, and good in everything."

–William Shakespeare

"Love is what I choose to build upon and build with. It's ecological, flexible, recyclable, organic, and forever self-sustaining."

–Jonathan J. Foster

For many years, when we lived in an unincorporated area of Northern California, my husband and I had a wood burning stove in our home. To warm the rooms, we had to keep the fire stoked. Larry bought cords of split firewood, or he and a friend cut down dead or over crowded branches of oak trees, then split the wood themselves.

Who doesn't enjoy a warm fire on a cold winter morning or night? Sitting in front of the comforting fireplace or stove, sipping cocoa, hot cider, or herbal tea, while enjoying a good book, may be your idea of a relaxing evening. But keeping that fire stoked has involved a lot of expense and sweat, maybe even sacrifice.

In the garden, we increase the heat of the compost pile by watering and stirring it regularly. Ideally, the pile of dry leaves, kitchen scraps, manure, garden trimmings, and even shredded paper will heat up and steam.

We publishers stoke the "fires" of interest and engagement of readers and potential readers. Fires tend to spread. Readers who are challenged, charmed, or changed by books will tell others about those books. Word of mouth is still the best publicity. To be effective and convincing, publicity must have the ring of authenticity and even spontaneity. Our part is to write and publish life changing books. And this only comes as you allow change in yourself, as you reach beyond yourself until your reach exceeds your grasp.

Let the seedbed of your own inner life be nourished until something transformative can gestate there. Be obedient to the vision. Be renewed in your calling morning by morning. Remember, God is with us! Be with God.

Wildfires are nature's way of renewing. When state forestry services haven't kept underbrush under control; when bark beetles have ravaged pine forests; when heavy rains encourage brush and grasses to burgeon beyond what is healthy and safe; when drought then dries the brush to brittle kindling that the smallest spark can ignite; then a firestorm is fed.

Living in California and now in Colorado, I have seen mighty, devastating, and frightening wildfires. My husband worked as a forest fire fighter between high school and college, in the Redwood region of Northern California.

We have witnessed tragic human losses, suffering wildlife, devastated vegetation. But wildfires clear forests of beetle-killed and over-crowded trees that pose dangers to people, wildlife, and streams. And come spring, wildflowers that haven't been seen for decades, bloom again. Eventually seedlings arise, new groves of trees develop, rivers run freely again, and wildlife flourish.

Rebuilding and new growth take time. But they come. And, wonderfully, out of the fearsome fiery force of nature comes renewal. As Dennis Ellingson explains in *God's Wild Herbs*, after fires wilderness meadows often fill with the wildflower Fireweed, so named because "its appearance is like that of dancing flames erupting from the forest floor."[70] These showy, vibrant pink or purple spiked flowers spring up first in an area that has been burned by wildfire. (Ellingson says ironically, the fluff from the pods is sometimes then used as tinder for starting campfires.)

Revival times have been called wildfires. They seem to spontaneously combust out of spiritually dry seasons, sparked by desire and prayer, and quickly spread. Flowers of renewed interest in prayer and worship spring up. Long-unseen miracles bloom. In such times writers and publishers have had a part in spreading the word with stories that spark hunger, ignite faith, and witness to the work of the Holy Spirit.

In publishing, book marketing, publicity, and sales there are times of deluge when books sell right and left. Then we labor through seasons of drought. In his book, *Sell Your Book Like Wildfire*, Rob Eager explains,

> Good writers will tell you that consistency is the key to honing their craft. Likewise, good marketers will tell you that consistency is the key to reaching a larger audience.... My desire is to help you light a fire under your marketing plan, get your book in front of more people, create a word-of-mouth wildfire, and enjoy the response of happy readers.[71]

A small-press publisher can deplete their resources with paid advertising, which comes with no guarantee of sales. There are many free or low-cost promotional activities that may be more gradual in getting the word out but are also more sustainable in continuing to reach new readers.

Our God who gives a vision also gives the provision. So go forth and share the vision and the message every authentic, organic way you can!

Let your writing and your marketing flow out of your life. Be attentive to what is near you, but not with *you* as the center; with *Christ* as the center within you, within history, in tradition, in the church, in the scriptures, in the world. People are looking for something, including books, which give meaning to their lives. People don't want to be preached at. They want to be seen, heard, cared about, and helped.

Think of marketing not as selling yourself or your book, but as communication. Communicate using every means at your disposal. Put as much effort into creatively communicating the existence and gist of your book as you put into writing the book content itself.

Remember that you are more than a writer/author or

publisher. An integrated life is a more purposeful, authentic, convincing life. Your book is one part of your ministry/calling. It can open doors and it can complement the other facets of your ministry, whether it is speaking, teaching, podcasting, blogging, joining and influencing conversations on social media, etc. Your book is one way to be part of the important dialogs humans are engaged in these days. No successful book author is *just* a book author.

What marketing strategies have worked for introverted Cladach authors? I'll share a few examples:

Dennis Ellingson

Though he's naturally outgoing, Dennis says hearing loss turned him into a "wall flower." First, as a Salvation Army worker and minister, he developed his interest in nature and herbs into an expertise. He researched, grew, foraged, used, and cooked with herbs. He wrote *God's Healing Herbs* and *God's Wild Herbs*. He took every opportunity to connect with readers and retailers, introducing his books to local bookstores, gift shops, and museum stores. For years he maintained an author page on Facebook as "The Herb Guy" and grew a following of 5,000 (with lots of engagement) by sharing daily tips and inspiration. He did what he loved: connecting with people around his two favorite subjects and expertise: encouraging people in their faith and sharing tips for healthy living and eating. He became a trusted friend and go-to expert to people who buy his books. Dennis also displayed and sold his books and herb products at outdoor festivals in Southern Oregon in summer. Then during winters in Arizona, he led "Herbs of the Bible" walking tours at a local arboretum, where his books sold in the gift shop.

Judith Galblum Pex

Judy may not fit the stereotypical introvert label, either,

but she says compared to her extremely outgoing husband, John, she is introverted. Living as a Christian in Israel makes her careful, if not reserved. She uses every connection she has, though, which are many through her and her husband's ministry and outreach. John and Judy run a hostel in the resort town Eilat, where they host thousands of people a year. She presents her books, including *Walk the Land: A Journey on Foot to Israel* to interested trail walkers, groups, and visitors. She has made contacts that have resulted in the publication of Hebrew, Dutch, and German translations of her books. The Pexes recently walked trails of the Camino de Santiago in Portugal and Spain. On the way they met other pilgrims, befriended them, and shared bookmarks about Judy's books.

Susan Bulanda

Sue also lives with hearing loss and other health issues in later life, which hinder her in face-to-face connections, she says. But, as a recognized expert in her field—an animal behaviorist and search-and-rescue dog trainer—she has garnered numerous endorsements and author interviews. She writes articles, blog posts, continues to publish books, and is generous in her willingness to publish reviews of other authors' books. She is good at keeping in touch with her publisher and working in conjunction with us to publicize the two books of hers that we publish: *God's Creatures: A Biblical View of Animals* and *Faithful Friends* (true stories of Jewish children who had to leave their pets behind during the Holocaust).

John Buzzard

John is downright shy. But he loves to write and has consistently worked to develop his talent. We first published his pull-no-punches memoir *Storm Tossed: How a U.S. Serviceman Won the Battle of Sex Addiction* under a pseudonym. John's confidence grew. He researched and wrote a strong work of historical fiction, *That Day by the Creek: A Novel about the Sand Creek Massacre of 1864* under his own name. This novel was a finalist for a *Foreword Magazine* award. John was encouraged, and since he loves researching the old west, he now writes a line of genre Westerns, which has won him a following by readers of that genre on the Amazon Kindle platform. The publisher of those genre Westerns interviewed John on radio and included him in local booksigning events. We are pleased to have helped John get his start.

Janyne McConnaughey

Janyne is another person we helped get started as an author. At 61 she quit her work as a Bible College professor so she could heal from childhood trauma. During intense psychotherapy, she says she "wrote her way to healing." When I approached her about publishing her story, she said I "was a godsend" because she wasn't sure she would have had the energy and courage to bring her story to print. We have published her three books of memoirs that have *Brave* in the title. Her books have reached and helped many readers, and they have helped her grow a platform for continued writing and speaking. She joined the leadership of the Attachment and Trauma Network, networked with church leaders, therapists, and educators, speaking at conferences, appearing on podcasts and radio interviews. And she continues to help others heal from childhood trauma, as well as help educators and ministers understand those among their students and congregants who are affected by trauma.

Gayle M. Irwin

I met Gayle at the Colorado Christian Writers Conference. Though not introverted she is somewhat hindered, she says, by living in Wyoming where "there are more pronghorn antelope than people." But she creates connections and opportunities and drives her little car to venues in Wyoming, Montana, and Northern Colorado. She joined a group of writers and authors who schedule book signings and other events together. A journalist by training, she writes regularly for a local paper. She used her experience as a wildlife journalist and work with rescue dogs in writing *Walking in Trust: Lessons Learned with my Blind Dog*. And her books keep selling.

Carol O'Casey
As a field biologist, Carol would rather be out in the forest, the desert, or the estuary observing, experiencing, and writing about nature and its Creator. But as a pastor's wife and a teacher, she learned (of necessity) to connect effectively with people. Her passion and expertise in her subject have compelled her to walk through the doors that open. The nature conservation and creation care organization A Rocha uses her book, *Unwrapping Wonder: Finding Hope in the Gift of Nature* in their nature curriculum.

Marilyn Bay
Marilyn is both a local Colorado sheep farmer and an experienced, traveled journalist. Her book, *All We Like Sheep: Lessons from the Sheepfold*, co-authored with her shepherdess mother, continues to sell year by year—because it is so authentic and real. The beautiful photo of pasture-grazing sheep on the cover doesn't hurt either! The value-added features help also: "Question to Ponder" and a prayer at the end of each chapter, with Glossary and Index of Scriptures at the back of the book.

For you writers I offer the above as examples. Follow the path that opens before *you*. And you, faith-based publishers, are directly or indirectly, whether centered or bounded (see Chapter 2), publishing glad tidings. If we hope to encourage and stoke renewed minds, lighter steps, warmed hearts, then we need to keep *ourselves* stoked—through community, education, and spiritual renewal practices.

Both writers and publishers: add fuel to your publishing program with new projects. Stoke the readers, and potential readers and community members, with reasons to buy, read, participate. Take your garden produce to market, so to speak. Put up signs, set up a fruit stand, enter vegetable and flowers in the county fair, give them to neighbors and to local food banks. Feed hungry people. Show hospitality. Welcome people into your garden. Create community.

Similarly, we sell and share books. There was a day when a book publisher or bookseller would go to work downtown in the morning. She would open the shop, greet the staff, inspect the shelves. Later she might leave the staff in charge and walk to the corner to buy a newspaper then sit down to read it at the coffee shop. While drinking a steaming cup, she would converse with other businesspeople and make new acquaintances. She might have with her a new book just released. She would show it to the people she meets (and drop it off at the local newspaper office to be reviewed in the paper). Then she would stroll back to her workplace for a day of creative output, editorial work, answering mail, business meetings, brainstorming, and decision making.

The publishing landscape looks different today, but we do the same things. Instead of driving or taking a bus downtown, I turn on my computer. I open email. I check the "shelves" on my website and the sales in our "store." I deal with questions, problems, enquiries, or book orders that come through email, text messages, or WhatsApp. Then I go to social media and visit with neighbors, other businesspeople, and friends, often making new connections and acquaintances. I show people the new titles we have for sale. We talk about the books we're reading. I find out what the political chatter is today. I peruse headlines for local and world events of interest. Often, I sip coffee or tea.

Just as important today, though they may look different, are community mindedness, keeping up relationships, taking time to interact, listen, learn, and share with others.

Even though you consider your writing and/or publishing a ministry, you must give attention to the business side to keep your ministry going. A small, Indie publisher can be much more flexible than large publishers. Use that advantage to adjust with alacrity to changing conditions, such as developments in production, distribution, materials availability, and cost increases.

In Chapter Two of this book, I shared the things I learned from my preacher father that have helped me be a better writer and publisher. Here are a few more:

1. The importance of knowing your readers and followers

My father made it a practice (it was a different day and age) to call on his flock in their homes regularly and to be there whenever trouble hit a family. He would stop by their businesses, farms, and workplaces for a friendly chat. When he stood in the pulpit to preach on Sunday, he knew those people. He knew their families, their joys and sorrows, the challenges they faced. He also knew their interests, their hobbies, what made them laugh or cry.

2. How to recruit, train, and encourage workers

The work and mission of the church needed people of all abilities and ages (and still does). I saw discernment in operation, encouragement expressed, and responsibilities entrusted. Organizing, scheduling, holding meetings were necessary. But loving God and loving people mattered most. Whether or not I heard that expressed in so many words, I definitely "caught" the mindset. As a writer and publisher I want to see increased sales and distribution. I want well-edited and designed books, I want engaged authors, reliable print providers, and enthusiastic book reviewers. I want readers to be encouraged, enlightened, and entertained by our books. But most of all I want to experience God's presence in all we do. I want to always remember that what we publish truly is "glad tidings."

3. The power of telling a story

My dad illustrated his sermons with stories that held the listeners' rapt attention. Often, he told stories of growing up on the farm or serving in the army at the end of WWII, on Okinawa or in South Korea. As I mentioned in an earlier chapter, I remember evangelists and camp meeting preachers who were great orators, spellbinding storytellers. Sometimes whole sermons were retelling of Bible stories full of drama that effectively drove home their message.

You, also, can hit home with your message by telling a good story. Every author has a story. Every book has a story. In fact, a popular and effective journalistic style today is creative nonfiction, which involves using fiction techniques in nonfiction writing.

My brother-in-law was a keen storyteller with a twinkle in his eyes. He told of childhood days visiting his aunt's Ohio farm. He'd go out on chilly mornings—barefoot and shivering—to bring in the cows for milking. To keep his feet warm (he said this with a winking grin) he would hop from one fresh, warm cowpie to the next.

My husband has his own cowpie story. When fighting forest fires in areas of range grazed cattle, he learned that dry cowpie piles would catch fire and burn for a long time. Even when the firefighters came into the area after the fire had gone through and left everything on the ground charred but no longer burning, a large cowpie could still be smoldering so hot that it would burn a hole through a water hose if they weren't careful. The fire fighters had to hold water hoses off the ground. Water was too precious to let that happen.

※

Some books seem to catch fire and burn hotter than others. It is interesting to see how different books sell better through different sales channels. Some sell consistently through wholesalers, others simply don't, but they sell well on Amazon. Some titles are mostly sold directly to the authors, who have ways of selling direct to customers. We give authors a generous discount, so they can make a lot more money on these sales than they can make with royalty income from Cladach's sales. It's a win-win, and most importantly, hope-giving books reach readers.

Bringing a book to publication has been compared to birthing a baby. There are many details, many concerns, many uncertainties, and a lot of anticipation during those nine months. Complications may arise. We wait, pray, prepare. We must be patient with the process.

Three times I have been present at the birth of a grandbaby, and I remember well the intensity, nervousness, and thrill. One can almost hear the flutter of angel wings and the ringing of heavenly bells as breath comes to this new life.... Nothing quite compares.

But birthing a book may come close. We dream and conceive, we learn to be patient through the gestation period as we write and wait, write and listen, write and pray, write and then rewrite, edit and polish.

Writers submit queries and proposals and manuscripts, then wait … and wait some more. Publishers agree, then prepare to attend the birth and catch the baby, wrap it in a bright cover, and hold it up in presentation to the world.

We feel as proud as new parents and full of wonder at the creation of this new thing. We have high hopes for this book baby, that it will thrive, that others will love and celebrate it with us, and that it will develop a growing circle of influence to make the world a better place; that it will help God's kingdom come, God's will be done on earth, as it is in Heaven.

We get excited when others notice our book baby. We appreciate every single person, famous or not, who posts a review of one of our titles, shares an update from one of our authors, and recommends a book to their friends and followers. Word of mouth is the most effective way of "getting the buzz going." Buzz gets people's attention. And well-written, hope-filled, evocative and provocative books are worth their attention.

As we do with our grown children, we release our books to the world. As a publisher, I love to hear stories of how our titles have found their way into every corner of the world and into the hands of readers. I occasionally hear from authors with stories like the following.

From Judy Pex:

> Last night in the Shelter an ultra-orthodox [Jewish] man—with a long beard and dressed in black—about our age, checked in and wanted to talk to John and me about the Israel Trail. He was not in the usual age category of hikers who stay at our shelter, and it is unusual to find an ultra-orthodox walking the Trail. He's from England and turns out he already read *Walk The Land* in English and even quoted bits of it. Now he plans to walk the Trail for a few days and had some specific questions about water, sleeping, etc. After talking for

about 45 minutes, John asked him what he thought about the spiritual parts of the book. He answered diplomatically that we had our differences. But it was an interesting conversation and contact.[72]

Two stories from Susan Jenkins:

> First, an old friend back in high school found me on Facebook and we got together for coffee. She told me that she was attending a women's conference in Texas a couple of years ago and *Scandalon* was offered as one of the books to buy. She bought it and then realized that I was the one who wrote it. As it turns out, she told me that her parents didn't allow her to attend church back in high school, but she came to my dad's church once with her next-door neighbor. As a result of that service she became a Christian. A few years later, she married a pastor and has been a pastor's wife for decades.
>
> The second story is from one of my former students in southern China, Muti. Muti wrote me recently and told me he was walking along a street in Hong Kong, and on a shelf outside a bookstore was *Scandalon*. He talked with the bookstore owner and she told him she liked the book because of the stories about China. So, of course, he bought a copy.[73]

Whether they find their way to Texas, Hong Kong, England, or Israel—what a joy and privilege to publish books that share good tidings. As a writer and publisher, you continue to broadcast seed and trust the holy breezes to carry it. There may be receptive soil in surprising places.

Looking back, we're amazed at what God has done—in, through, and with us, our authors, and our books—as we have sought to share stories and other writings that show God at work in our world, and that show people getting involved and working with God. We believe now more than ever that God is present and working for good everywhere, all the time, now and forever!

Having done all, stand in the garden. You aren't in a competition; you are contributing to the conversation, a voice that needs to be heard. Don't gloat over your prolific Spirea. But float the next terrific idea. Think Spring. Use emerging means. Use ingenuity, opportunity, and technology to reach readers and share your message. Watch the "weather"; work with the seasons. In gardening and farming, timing is "everything." Same with publishing. But "publish glad tidings" in season and out. The harvest will come.

APPENDIX I

PUBLISHING MODELS

A good resource for understanding many of the publishing models available today, is Jane Friedman's "Publishing Paths" chart that she makes available free here:

https://janefriedman.com/key-book-publishing-path/

Jane lists the following paths to publishing a book:

1. Traditional

This category includes the Big Five New York houses and other large corporate houses/imprints. They have sales teams that meet with major retailers, wholesalers, and libraries. Most books are sold months in advance and shipped for a specific release date. Nearly every book has a print run; print-on-demand is used when stock runs low or sales dwindle.

The books have mainstream appeal and most of the authors have significant platforms.

Jane gives this advice to authors concerning traditional publishers:

- Most advances do not earn out.
- Publishers holds publishing rights for all major formats indefinitely.
- Authors don't control title or cover design.
- Authors are often unhappy with marketing support or surprised at lack of support.

2. Small Press

This category is harder to define. The term "small press" means different things to different people. Jane uses it to describe publishers that avoid both advances and print runs. They take on less financial risk than traditional publishers do.

Authors receive no advance or possibly a token advance. Royalty rates may look the same as a traditional publisher's or be more favorable since the publisher has less financial risk upfront. Many rely on sales and discovery through Amazon; others may focus on direct-to-consumer sales and marketing or specialty sales. A handful of small presses may sell into the bookstore market if they have a distributor. Some rely entirely on the author's efforts to market and publicize their books. However, well-established small presses' editorial, design, and marketing support equals that of larger houses.

However, Jane warns:

- The quality of work may be low.
- Don't expect print/bookstore distribution if the press uses print-on-demand. (Ask!)
- Such presses may rely on authors to sell or blame authors for poor sales.
- Avoid rights grabs; reserve some subsidiary rights.

3. Assisted and Hybrid

Hybrid publishers work like traditional publishers in that they put their name and one of their ISBNs on your book. Assisted publishing services, on the other hand, may or may not do this—and they may even offer you a choice of using theirs or your own.

Both hybrid and assisted services require the author to pay to publish. With most, selling books is up to the author.

Some offer paid marketing packages, assistance with the book launch, or paid promotional opportunities.

This model is ideal for authors with more money than time, but it is not a sustainable business model for career authors, says Jane. She warns:

- Some services call themselves "hybrid" because it sounds fashionable and savvy.
- Avoid companies that take advantage of author inexperience and use high-pressure sales tactics.

4. Indie or DIY Self-Publishing

The author manages the publishing process and may hire people/services to edit, design, print, and distribute. The author remains in complete control of all artistic and business decisions. Print-on-demand (POD, most often via Amazon KDP or IngramSpark) makes it affordable to sell and distribute print books through online retail. With printer-ready PDF files, it costs little or nothing to start.

If authors are confident about sales, they may hire a printer, invest in a print run, manage inventory, fulfillment, shipping, etc.

Jane warns:

- Authors may not invest enough money or time to produce a quality book or market it.
- Authors may not have the experience to know what quality help looks like or what it takes to produce a quality book.
- It is difficult for first-time authors to get mainstream reviews, media attention or sales through conventional channels (bookstores, libraries). But it can happen over time, if demand builds for the authors' work.

5. Social Publishing

With this model authors write, publish, and distribute work in a public or semi-public forum, directly for readers. Emphasis is on feedback and growth; sales or income can be rare. Categories include: Serialization, Fan Fiction, Social Media, and Patronage (such as Patreon and Substack).

Social publishing allows writers to develop an audience for their work, even while learning and improving their writing.

Many popular platforms include monetization methods, such as tipping/donations, ad revenue sharing, and premium content options for paying readers.

IBPA (the Independent Book Publishers Association) has developed their own chart of publishing models. The IBPA Publishing MAP, along with helpful explanations, may be downloaded free here:

https://www.ibpa-online.org/page/PublishingMAP

This chart includes eight publishing models:

1. Association, Society, & Non-Profit Publishers
2. Author Publishers
3. Corporate Trade Publishers
4. Higher Education & Academic Publishers
5. Hybrid Publishers
6. Independent Publishers & Small Presses
7. Service Providers
8. University Presses

APPENDIX II

THE PUBLISHING PROCESS

With whatever publishing model a book enters the world, the gestation and birth process involve many tasks. And a publisher wears many hats. I'll describe a few of them for you:

1. ACQUISITIONS

The publisher receives queries and proposals, depending on their policies, direct from prospective authors or indirectly through agents. The one wearing the acquisitions editor hat tries to answer them in a timely fashion, but sometimes queries "fall between the cracks" of slush piles, old emails, and busy days. This is a hard job if it's difficult for you to say "No." If an author and their query does pique the publisher's interest, they may ask for a full proposal and 1 to 3 sample chapters. Acquisitions editors may attend conferences to meet writers and find manuscripts to publish.

First impressions of an author or manuscript are inevitably subjective. The editor may like the person, writing, or idea based on personal preferences and interests or their persuasiveness and ability to engage readers through written expression.

If an author/book idea crosses that first threshold, it must then hold up under business scrutiny. Tough questions should be asked, analysis and forecasting applied: Is there enough demand for a book of this subject or genre? If so, can the publisher and author reach the market for this book? Is it unique enough to compete with similar books? Does it fit the publisher's niche?

With some projects we know that we are taking risks, a bit like testing new varieties of fruits and vegetables at the produce market. If we believe in an author's project, we may be willing to experiment with new seed types, soil amendments, perhaps try companion planting in our garden of books. If we take too many risks too often, though, we cannot stay in the publishing business/ministry.

Some book projects are introduced with excitement, but sales soon peter out. Other titles, like seeds carried by wind or birds, continue to find ready soil, and sell week after week, month after month, year after year. With the benefit of hindsight, I can see that the following factors make a difference in whether a book succeeds:

- What other titles has the author published? For instance, if their other titles are poorly edited self-published books, this author's reputation may suffer and hinder potential sales of the title we have carefully edited.
- How actively connected is the author with the book's prospective audience—even before publication?
- Is there a waiting audience/demand/hunger for this book?
- Does the author have a "platform," an ongoing means of reaching that audience? And/or is it an audience the publisher can reach?

In my mind this begs the question: "As a writer, when are

you ready to have your book published?"

Writers who feel they have something to say and long to be published authors, tend to become impatient. Don't let that happen. Your preparations to publish involve much more than finishing a manuscript and writing an effective book proposal. You also need to:

- Find/identify/make connections with and get to know the audience for your book. (Ideally you will start this ongoing process even before you write the manuscript.)
- Get your finances in order. It costs to publish and market effectively, even when you publish with a traditional (large, small, or micro) royalty publisher.
- Resolve, as far as you can, personal issues. Working as a published author takes time, energy, commitment, and the support of people around you.

I have accepted manuscripts that I personally liked so much that I was willing to risk not selling many copies, knowing it (likely poetry, literary fictions, or an anthology of thoughtful essays) would not be a general interest book. As John Thompson, author of *Merchants of Culture*, explains,

> Regardless of the differences in the beliefs and aspirations that motivate small publishers ... their smallness gives them a degree of freedom and creativity—they can be nimble, move quickly, experiment with unconventional books, or simply publish books they like.... But their smallness also renders them vulnerable in several ways.[74]

Thompson goes on to describe those vulnerabilities, three of which I have experienced: undercapitalization, difficulty getting media attention for their books, and dependence on a couple of highly successful books.

Back to the hats. After a publisher accepts a book proposal, there follow contract offers, negotiations, and agreements. From the very beginning it's important to consider the following:

2. MARKETING

Our main task, besides producing great books and making them available, is to create demand for those books. If we believe in each book's author, message, artfulness, and ability to touch hearts and minds, then we must continually look for ways to introduce and convince potential readers that these books will give them enjoyment as well as insight, encouragement, and inspiration. I share more on marketing in Chapter 5, "Stoke."

3. COPY EDITING

Manuscripts, drafts, proofs, whether digital or printed copies, all need editing. Either you or one of your staff—or an editor hired for the job—goes through each sentence, each line, each word with a fine-toothed comb, digging, refining, clarifying, cleaning up, and polishing. Many books first require content and structural editing.

4. INFORMATION MANAGEMENT

Once we upload the book's data to places like Bowker, Ingram, Amazon.com, BN.com, Baker & Taylor, and the Library of Congress, that information disseminates across the internet and in book data retrieval systems worldwide. It is important that this metadata be accurate, consistent, and kept up to date. Metadata includes title, byline, ISBN, price, book descriptions, back cover copy, review quotes, subject categories, key words (or search terms and phrases), and author bio.

5. FINANCIAL ANALYSIS

As book sales trickle in—and occasionally a bulk order comes knocking on our door unexpectedly—the plus side of the accounting spreadsheet increases and we try to forecast expenses and how many books to print, the best use of advertising/publicity budget (if there is one), what percent royalties and advances to offer authors, what retail prices to assign to a title, etc., etc. Profits aren't real impressively high, but Cladach stays in the black. We often remind ourselves that we are doing this as ministry. But to be sustained, ministry must be carried out in a businesslike way. The business side is often difficult for creatives and entrepreneurs to get their heads around or want to spend time on. I am fortunate that my husband, an accountant, has been managing that side of Cladach from the beginning.

6. SALES

With this hat on, one may call or visit a store to check sales, restock consignment shelves, or send mailings to announce new titles. This involves establishing accounts with book wholesalers and/or distributors. We receive direct orders from individuals, authors, stores, libraries, and nonprofits in the U.S., U.K., and beyond. My husband, Larry, processes the orders with accounting software, keeps meticulous and conscientious records, and produces regular sales reports.

7. BUSINESS MANAGEMENT

The buck stops here. Decisions must be made, staff meetings held (if one has a staff) and communications directed. I enjoy creative brainstorming.

8. CONTENT DEVELOPMENT

We create content for editorial and marketing purposes, to be shared as book descriptions, back cover copy, web pages, bios, blog posts, social media posts, videos, letters, newsletters, press releases, etc.

9. CONTENT CONVERSION

So we've written an article or post, we've developed and produced a paperback book, we've published a web page. Now we can convert the paperback file into an ebook file, the post into tweets, the graphics and description into a video trailer, the web page content into an ad or an email. Repurpose content. Get the idea?

10. SHIPPING/FULFILLMENT

Larry has expertly taken on this job and wears this hat almost daily. Our warehouse/shipping department is lined with cartons of books and is set up with packing supplies and a table surface for sorting, labeling, packing. Trips are made to the Post Office and to FedEx. This hat is fun to wear. We love sending out books! Go, team Cladach! (I should add, though, that the rise in shipping costs as well as printing costs have prompted our increasing use of print-on-demand.)

11. DESIGN

Here's an aspect of publishing that is challenging but fun and satisfying to the artistic side and creative urges of this publisher. But it can eat up time and requires a constant, steep learning curve. We use top of the line software to design book pages and covers. Many of our book covers have been designed in-house, but we have contracted with graphic designers and artists for cover designs and interior art. Besides the books themselves, there are web pages, promo pieces like postcards and sell sheets, and other design output. We keep this hat handy, usually near the computer.

12. PRINT BUYING

The book cover is designed and tweaked, the text edited and proofed, the pages formatted, the metadata uploaded and disseminated, the forthcoming title announced. The book must then be printed! This has often involved organizing and sending out print specifications, studying and comparing print quotes, comparing choices of papers, finishes, bindings. Decisions, decisions—often feeling like guesses—about how many books are expected to sell and how quickly, how active the author will be in promoting their book, how wide a market we can reach. Economies of scale come into play. Should we print a larger quantity and pay much less per copy and have a lot of stock on hand and use up our cash; or print a small quantity and preserve cash flow, though we pay much more per copy? Or should we go with print-on-demand? Once we've chosen the printer, the next decision is "how many books to print?"

13. SOCIAL MEDIA

This has become an important hat to wear at least a while each day. Social media is where readers are hanging out and we can connect and get acquainted and talk about some of our favorite things: ideas and experiences; the daily life of faith, work, family, and wonder; our Creator and Lord who initiates every good thing; creativity; new and talented authors; author and book events; opportunities; and … books! We connect with people through our website and blog, on Facebook, LinkedIn, Goodreads, and Twitter (now X). You will have your own list of what platforms work for you and that you enjoy.

APPENDIX III

MARKETING FOR INTROVERTS

> "Writing is something you do alone. It's a profession for introverts who want to tell you a story but don't want to make eye contact while doing it."
>
> –John Green

Many writers are somewhat introverted. But even they can happily, effectively, and successfully engage in marketing their books. Any author can connect with their audience, share their expertise, and grow a readership. John Kremer, author of *1001 Ways to Market Your Books*, says all it takes is to "produce a good book and let people know about it."

If I'm going to write a book, then I'm going to do my best to make sure that everyone who might benefit from the book gets a chance to read it. I believe that all writers and all publishers should be as committed to marketing their books.[75]

Writers and publishers are communicators. Ask: *What am I giving my audience, what need or desire am I addressing? What am I hoping to make them feel? Am I adding value to their lives? Am I giving them a good time by exercising hospitality? Am I providing them an experience of community?*

When do you start marketing? Authors need to start before they finish writing their book. (The publisher should start as soon as they agree to publish the book.) Author, know your audience and keep them in mind as you write. Share steps in the journey of writing and the publishing process on your blog or social media to keep your followers interested and feeling "in the loop." Think collaboratively; ask your followers for input. Join a local writer's group and online writer/author groups where you can have your questions answered, both give and receive support.

You can often build marketing tools into your book. For instance: Prepare a reader's guide or group discussion guide to include in the book (make it meaty, with discussable points, keep the wording simple and understandable. For fiction, even some nonfiction, you may want to add extras, such as recipes, a tour of the city (setting), etc.; or prepare such content for your blog posts.

Recruit a launch team. Plan a creative and enjoyable launch. Garner pre-orders to "get buzz going." Prepare a tip sheet with a list of the most interesting bits of information and/or quotes from your book. Add a catchy lead at the top and an "about the book" section at the bottom. This you can send to publications, sites, and blogs who may be interested in publishing your tips and mentioning your book in the process.

In sharing your book with the world, first give thought to how to present yourself. This involves an author bio, a website, and promotional materials. Most important: be real, sincere, and genuine.

Write your author bio (both short and long versions) in third person. Make it interesting, not too long. Read bios of authors you like. Keep your author photo and bio up to date. Include the latest information including any awards you have won, other books you have written, and author events.

List your online author presence, such as website, Amazon author page, Goodreads author page, Facebook, LinkedIn, Instagram, Twitter (or X), etc. (Use and have an active presence on the platforms that work for you, on which you feel comfortable, and where you can find your "tribe" or "target audience.") Take risks, be adventurous and friendly. Remember, contempt for new forms of communication will keep you from communicating what you have discovered, experienced, learned.

Think in terms of quality of followers, not just quantity. Social media is an "attention economy." The value of your platform is in how much attention people give to, dialogue with, respond to what you say (and vice versa; it won't work unless you also respond and show interest in them), not in how many thousands of followers or "friends" you have. Algorithms keep changing and can open doors and opportunities, but they also have their own agendas.

Be part of community, both in person and online. Nurture relationships based on mutual interests, respect, openness, and helpfulness.

All the while you are building your unique "brand" as you know and communicate your unique mission and vision.

Next, give thought to how to present your book. Let trusted readers (literary friends, critique partners, etc.) read and give feedback on your manuscript. Garner endorsements (at least some of which should be recognizable names or experts in the subject of your book) and schedule interviews. Guest blogging and guest appearances on podcasts are popular now.

One of the most effective ways to promote a book is through reviews. They give you and your book credibility; you can share review blurbs on social media and in printed sell sheets. Prospective readers and book browsers pay attention to reviews. Book reviewers and advance readers are an important element in the publishing process. It's hard for the author and the editors to be objective about the book they've been immersed in for months, maybe years. Enter readers and reviewers who usually have little or no personal stake or emotional involvement in the book. Reviewers can help us improve.

Whether you or someone else is the publisher, you can help create, maintain, and update your book's availability and metadata (which I defined in the Introduction).

To gain and connect effectively with readers, ask yourself where your potential readers hang out? Go there. Where do they spend time? What do they read? What do they value? How can you get their attention? Ultimately, people buy from those they know, like, and trust. Online active presence as well as personal appearances provide opportunities to build that sense of knowing and trusting. As you interact with people in person and on social media, along the way you will find "adjacent audiences" who are not aware of, but would be interested in, what you offer. You can also engage with your local independent bookstores and libraries.

Another way to promote your book is to create shareable content. Share passages from your book or other writing. Write and share auxiliary content, background material, etc.

Many leading voices are telling us the best method of building and reaching and keeping in touch with your followers and readers is personal and direct: "good old fashioned" email. Marketing expert, Jane Friedman, considers e-mail the most effective marketing tool.

Even introverted authors need to engage occasionally through in-person events. Many pastors of churches are introverted people, but they get up and preach every Sunday, because they love God, the Word of God, and people. True, most people are primarily one or the other: a speaker or a writer. But you can learn to exercise a lesser gift for the sake of the stronger gift. Seek and accept speaking, workshop, book talk, or book signing opportunities whenever you can.

Most important, keep writing! Share your expertise, passion, creativity, vision. Repurpose content and/or exercise subsidiary rights. Write reviews and endorsements for other authors and their books. Enter your books in appropriate contests. It doesn't have to be the Pulitzer Prize. For instance, we have a book that won the Dog Writers Association award, and a novel that won the Bay Area Independent Publishers award for best inspirational novel, and another novel was a finalist in a *Foreword Magazine* book of the year award.

Author marketing and platform development involve 1) Being yourself and 2) Connecting authentically and helpfully with readers. Say yes to opportunities. Share generously and graciously.

If you do the above (and there are many helps available for author branding and book marketing), no efforts will be wasted. Do something every day, if possible. I consistently see a correlation between author efforts and book sales. When I notice a title spike in sales, I am not surprised when the author mentions that they spoke at a conference, or did a book talk at a library or a signing at a local store, or published an article in a magazine, or were interviewed on a podcast. When an author promotes and engages, their book sells better. It's that simple.

NOTES

1. Quoted from "Esther Meek on Hope and the Struggle to Trust that Being is Good and Reality is a Gift," The Meaning Code Youtube Channel, Apr 29, 2022, accessed at https://www.youtube.com/watch?v=q7VR-PXGoAs

2. Madeleine L'Engle, *Bright Evening Star: Mystery of the Incarnation* (Colorado Springs: Waterbrook Press, 1997), 14.

3. Cathy Lynn Grossman, "How Religion Publishing Became a Billion Dollar Industry," *Publisher's Weekly* (April 19, 2022), Accessed at: https://www.publishersweekly.com/pw/by-topic/industry-news/religion/article/89000-how-religion-publishing-became-a-billion-dollar-industry.html

4. My author friend Alice Scott-Ferguson, whose faith journey can be read in her memoir, *Daughter of the Isles*, sent me this description (in an email) of the DONES (with whom she identifies) and of the NONES:

> "The DONES are those who no longer appear in the building but who are a large global community of those who have become disillusioned with the system, but not with their God. They are vocal and influential in opening up fresh aspects of biblical interpretation. They are not all necessarily connected with one another but are challenging the status quo in many different ways, with one common tenet: Re-examining the Scriptures under the light of the Spirit, *the* great and only teacher. In other words, unlocking the Bible through the lens of Christ. There are new publishing houses opening to cater to this demographic of readers and writers. I count myself in this tribe.
>
> "The NONES claim devout spirituality with no

traditional religious background. I think we have much in common in our quest for connection to One Greater and to live a life of love that has jettisoned judgement. As a demographic, literature for this group is a wide open field in which to plant the seed of the Source of all the attributes to which they aspire."

5. James A. Michener, *Centennial* (Random House, 1974).

6. Psalm 89:36-37; 90:2 (KJV)

7. Phyllis Tickle, *The Great Emergence: How Christianity Is Changing and Why* (Baker, 2008), 84-5.

8. Tickle, pp. 96-97.

9. Rod Dreher, *The Benedict Option: A Strategy for Christians In a Post-Christian Nation* (Penguin Random House, 2017)

10. Robert N. Bellah, Richard Madsen, William M. Sullivan, Ann Swidler, and Steven M. Tipton, *Habits of the Heart: Individualism and Commitment in American Life* (University of California Press, 1985), 135.

11. Tickle, 152-3.

12. Tickle, 160.

13. Diana Butler Bass, *Grounded: Finding God In the World: A Spiritual Revolution* (HarperCollins, 2015), 15.

14. Bass, 121.

15. William J. Abraham, *The Coming Great Revival: Recovering the Full Evangelical Tradition* (Harper & Row, 1984), 55.

16. Brian D. McClaren, *The Great Spiritual Migration: How the World's Largest Religion Is Seeking a Better Way to Be Christian* (New York: Convergent, 2016), 5-6.

17. Ed Cyzewski, *Pray, Write, Grow: Cultivating Prayer and Writing Together* (Independently Published, 2015), accessed in ebook version.

18. Dennis Linn, Sheila Fabricant Linn, and Matthew Linn SJ, *Sleeping with Bread: Holding What Gives You Life* (Paulist Press, 1995).

19. Psalm 23:2-3

20. Carol O'Casey, *Unwrapping Wonder: Finding Hope in the Gift of Nature* (Cladach, 2013), 11.

21. Bruce Epperly, "Writing with God" in *Partnering with God: Exploring Collaboration in Open and Relational Theology* (SacraSage, 2021), 257-8.

22. Robert Barron, *Redeeming the Time: Gospel Perspectives on the Challenges of the Hour* (Word on Fire, 2022), 277-8.

23. Tickle, p.160.

24. Emily A. Pastor, @emilyannepastor replying to @_the_last_echo on Twitter (X), 11/8/22.

25. William Zinsser, *On Writing Well: An Informal Guide to Writing Nonfiction* (Harper & Row, On Writing Well, 1976), 6.

26. Nancy Swihart, *On Kitten Creek: Searching for the Sacred* (Cladach, 2017), 129.

27. George Orwell, "Politics and the English Language," *Writer to Writer: Readings on the Craft of Writing* (Houghton Mifflin, 1966), 202.

28. Epperly, 258.

29. Stanley J. Grenz, *A Primer on Postmodernism* (Grand Rapids: Eerdmans, 1996), 10.

30. Jonathan Foster in an email correspondence

31. Jurgen Moltmann, *God In Creation: A New Theology of Creation and the Spirit of God* (Fortress, 1993), 310-11.

32. Jonathan Foster in an email correspondence

33. Michael Card, "God's Own Fool" song lyrics (Birdwing Music and Mole End Music, 1986).

34. Gary Hassig, *Contemplation: Only the Crucified Are Truly Alive: An Ancient Practice for the 21st Century* (Colorado Springs: StarHolder, 2014), 208-9.

35. Peter Enns, *The Sin of Certainty: Why God Desires Our Trust*

More Than Our "Correct" Beliefs, audiobook version (Tantor Audio 2016: HarperOne, 2016), at 13:00 and 24:00.

36. Ibid.

37. Grenz, 164-5.

38. Catherine Lawton, *Remembering Softly: A Life in Poems* (Cladach, 2018), 15.

39. Grenz, 110.

40. Zinsser, 35.

41. Psalm 42:7

42. Malcolm Guite, *Lifting the Veil: Imagination and the Kingdom of God* (Square Halo Books, 2021), 27.

43. N.T. Wright, *God and the Pandemic: A Christian Reflection on the Coronavirus and its Aftermath* (Zondervan, 2020), 48-51.

44. Paul Antleitner. "The God We Thought Was Dead," *Ekstasis Magazine* (February 16, 2022), Accessed at: https://www.ekstasismagazine.com/blog/2022/2/16/the-god-we-thought-was-dead/

45. Barron, *Redeeming the Time*, pp. 26-28.

46. Leonard Cohen, "Anthem," song lyrics © Stranger Music Inc.

47. Philip Yancey on Carey Nieuwhof leadership podcast, March 1, 2022. Accessed at: https://m.youtube.com/watch?v=ZjRGaOBvD7g

48. Peterson, *Adorning the Dark*, p. 73

49. Dialogue from the movie, *The Lord of the Rings: The Return of the King*. Script accessed at: https://imsdb.com/scripts/Lord-of-the-Rings-Return-of-the-King.html

50. Ibid.

51. Peterson, *Adorning the Dark*, p. 191-192

52. O'Casey, email.

53. L'Engle, *Walking on Water,* p.67

54. Madeleine L'Engle, *A Cry Like a Bell: Poems* (Harold Shaw, 1987), 58.

55. McEntyre, p. 2.

56. Tim Reddish, *Does God Always Get What God Wants?: An Exploration of God's Activity in a Suffering World* (Eugene: Cascxade Books, 2018), xiv.

57. Thomas Jay Oord, *Open and Relational Theology: An Introduction To Life-Changing Ideas* (SacraSage, 2021), 91-93.

58. Catherine Keller, *On the Mystery: Discerning Divinity In Process* (Fortress Press, 2008), 15.

59. Robert Barron, "The Question Behind the Question." *Redeeming the Time.* (Word on Fire, 2022), 256.

60. Bradley Jersak, *A More Christlike God: A More Beautiful Gospel* (Plain Truth Ministries, 2015), 145, 152.

61. Robert Barron, "The Parable of the Sower and You" in *The Word on Fire Bible: The Gospels* (Word on Fire, 2020), 85.

62. Patricia Adams Farmer, *Embracing a Beautiful God* (St. Louis: Chalice Press, 2003), 41.

63. Thomas Jay Oord, "Imitate God—Take Risks!" Blog post (June 29, 2010). Accessed at: https://thomasjayoord.com/index.php/blog/archives/imitate_god_-_take_risks/

64. D.C. Schindler, *Love and the Postmodern Predicament* (Cascade, 2018), p. 22.

65. Jay McDaniel, *What Is Process Thought?: Seven Answers to Seven Questions* (Process Century Press, 2021), p. 66.

66. Jurgen Moltmann, *Theology of Hope*, trans. James W. Leitch (London: SCM Press, 2002), 313.

67. Richard Rohr, *Essential Teachings on Love* (Maryknoll: Orbis Books, 2018), 132.

68. Thomas Merton, *No Man Is an Island.* Ebook version. (New York: Houghton Mifflin Harcourt, 1983), at 78%.

69. Barron, *Redeeming*, p.39.

70. Dennis Ellingson, *God's Wild Herbs: Identifying and Using 121 Plants Found in the Wild* (Cladach, 2010), 56.

71. Rob Eager, *Sell Your Book Like Wildfire: The Writer's Guide to Marketing & Publicity* (F+W Media, 2012), 3.

72. Personal note.

73. Personal note.

74. John B. Thompson, *Merchants of Culture: The Publishing Business in the Twenty-First Century* (New York: Penguin Group, 2012), 162.

75. John Kremer, *1001 Ways to Market Your Books*, Real World Edition. Kindle Edition. (Open Horizons, 2016), Introduction.

BIBLIOGRAPHY

Arnold, Allen. *The Story of WITH: A Better Way to Live, Love, & Create.* Independently Published, 2016.

Barron, Robert. *Redeeming the Time: Gospel Perspectives on the Challenges of the Heart.* Park Ridge: Word on Fire, 2022.

———. *The Word On Fire Bible: The Gospels.* Word on Fire, 2020.

Bass, Diana Butler. *Grounded: Finding God in the World, A Spiritual Revolution.* New York: Harper Collins, 2015.

———. *Christianity After Religion: The End of Church and the Birth of a New Spiritual Awakening.* HarperOne, 2012.

Bellah, Robert N., Richard Madsen, William M. Sullivan, Ann Swidler, Steven M. Tipton. *Habits of the Heart: Individualism and Commitment in American Life.* University of California Press, 1985.

Biel, Joe. *A People's Guide to Publishing: Build a Successful, Sustainable, Meaningful, Book Business from the Ground Up.* Portland: Microcosm, 2018.

Cyzewski, Ed. *Pray, Write, Grow: Cultivating Prayer and Writing Together.* Independently Published, 2015.

———. *The Contemplative Writer: Loving God through Christian Spirituality, Meditation, Daily Prayer, and Writing.* Independently Published, 2016.

Eagar, Rob. *Sell Your Book Like Wildfire: The Writer's Guide to Marketing and Publicity*. Cincinnati: Writers Digest Books, 2012.

Enns, Peter. *The Sin of Certainty: Why God Desires Our Trust More Than Our "Correct" Beliefs*. Tantor Audio, 2016; HarperOne, 2016.

Farmer, Patricia Adams. *Embracing a Beautiful God*. St. Louis: Chalice Press, 2003.

Foster, Jonathan. *The Reconstructionist*. Oak Glen: Quoir, 2021.

Gallagher, Susan V. and Roger Lundin. *Literature Through the Eyes of Faith*. San Francisco: HarperCollins, 1989.

Grenz, Stanley J. *A Primer on Postmodernism*. Grand Rapids: Eerdmans, 1996.

Grossman, Cathy Lynn. "Publishing's Spirituality Sector Grows." In *Publishers Weekly*, Mar 18, 2022.

Guite, Malcolm. *The Word Within the Words*. Minneapolis: Fortress Press, 2022.

———. *Lifting the Veil: Imagination and the Kingdom of God*. Square Halo Books, 2021.

Gutkind, Lee. *You Can't Make This Stuff Up: The Complete Guide to Writing Creative Nonfiction from Memoir to Literary Journalism and Everything In Between*. Da Capo Press, 2012.

Huebner, Erinn (2018) "A History of Christian Publishing," *The Christian Librarian*: Vol. 61 : Iss. 1, Article 8. Available at: http://digitalcommons.georgefox.edu/tcl/vol61/iss1/8

Jersak, Brad. *Can You Hear Me?: Tuning In to the God Who Speaks*. Abbotsford: Fresh Wind Press, 2003, 2012.

———. *A More Christlike God: A More Beautiful Gospel*. Pasadena: Plain Truth Ministries, 2015.

Keller, Catherine. *On the Mystery: Discerning Divinity In Process*. Minneapolis: Fortress Press, 2008.

Kremer, John. *1001 Ways to Market Your Books: for Authors and Publishers*. Open Horizons, 1998.

L'Engle, Madeleine. *Bright Evening Star: Mystery of the Incarnation*. New York: Convergent, 2018.

———. *Walking on Water: Reflections on Faith and Art*. New York: Bantam, 1980.

MacDonald, George. *Unspoken Sermons*: Series I, II, and III. Start Publishing LLC, 2012.

McDaniel, Jay. *What Is Process Thought?: Seven Answers to Seven Questions*. Process Century Press, 2021.

McLaren, Brian D. *A Generous Orthodoxy: Why I am a missional, evangelical, post/protestant, liberal / conservative, mystical / poetic, biblical, charismatic / contemplative, fundamentalist / calvinist, anabaptist / anglican, methodist, catholic, green, incarnational, depressed — yet hopeful, emergent, unfinished Christian*. Grand Rapids: Zondervan, 2006.

———. *The Great Spiritual Migration: How the World's Largest Religion Is Seeking a Better Way to Be Christian*. Convergent, 2016.

McEntyre, Marilyn. *Speaking Peace in a Climate of Conflict*. Grand Rapids: Wm. B. Eerdmans, 2020.

Moltmann, Jürgen. *God in Creation: A Theology of Creation and the Spirit of God*. Minneapolis: Fortress Press, 1985, 1993.

———. *Theology of Hope*. Translated by James W. Leitch. London: SCM Press, 2002.

O'Connor, Flannery. *Mystery and Manners: Occasional Prose*. New York: Fitzgerald, Farrar, Straus and Giroux, 1962, 1994.

Oord, Thomas Jay. *Open and Relational Theology: An Introduction to Life-Changing Ideas*. SacraSage Press, 2021.

Peterson, Andrew. *Adorning the Dark: Thoughts on Community, Calling, and the Mystery of Making*. Nashville: B&H Publishing, 2019.

Reddish, Tim. *Does God Always Get What God Wants?: An Exploration of God's Activity in a Suffering World*. Cascade Books, 2018.

——— and Bonnie Rambob, Fran Stedman, and Thomas Jay Oord, eds. *Partnering with God: Exploring Collaboration in Open and Relational Theology*. SacraSage Press, 2021.

Rodale, J.I. *How to Grow Vegetables and Fruits by the Organic Method*. Rodale Press, 1977.

Rohr, Richard. *Essential Teachings on Love*. Maryknoll: Orbis Books, 2018.

———. *The Divine Dance: The Trinity and Your Transformation*. New Kensington: Whitaker House, 2016.

Schindler, D. C. *Love and the Postmodern Predicament: Rediscovering the Real in Beauty, Goodness, and Truth*. Eugene: Wipf and Stock, 2018.

Smith, Datus C., Jr. *A Guide to Book Publishing*. Revised Edition. Seattle and London: University of Washington Press, 1989.

Swenson, Allan A. *The Practical Book of Organic Gardening*. Universal-Tandem, 1973.

Thompson, John B. *Book Wars: The Digital Revolution in Publishing*. Medford and Cambridge: Polity Press, 2021.

———. *Merchants of Culture: The Publishing Business in the Twenty-First Century*. Second Edition. London and New York: Penguin, 2012.

Tickle, Phyllis. *The Great Emergence: How Christianity Is Changing and Why*. Grand Rapids: Baker Books, 2008.

Watkins, Floyd C. and Knight, Karl F., *Writer to Writer: Readings on the Craft of Writing*. Houghton Mifflin, 1966.

Willard, Dallas. *Hearing God: Developing a Conversational Relationship with God*. Downers Grove: InterVarsity Press, 1984,1999.

Wright, N.T. *God and the Pandemic: A Christian Reflection on the Coronavirus and its Aftermath*. Zondervan, 2020.

———, *Surprised by Hope: Rethinking Heaven, the Resurrection, and the Mission of the Church*. New York: HarperCollins, 2008.

Zinsser, William. *On Writing Well: An Informal Guide to Writing Nonfiction*. Harper & Row, 1976.

ACKNOWLEDGMENTS

This book didn't germinate and grow in wilderness wasteland. Many others helped feed my roots, gave input directly, and encouraged my growth and efforts at articulation. These include the authors of the books and articles I quote, the pre-publication readers, and my personal and professional teachers and mentors through the years.

I want to especially thank Rev. Dr. Robert Duncan of Northwind Theological Seminary for affirming and encouraging me in creatively presenting and sharing my research and experience for other writers and publishers, and to think of it all as ministry.

Then there's theological writer and editor Jonathan Foster who read the manuscript and made suggestions for pruning and mulching and cultivating some of my thinking and wording (you might say) to make it more tasty and digestible.

My thanks also to author and publisher Marlene Bagnull for giving me opportunities to teach from this material at the Christian writers conferences she directs.

Heartfelt thanks to all the writers I have worked with and whose books I have published in the past twenty-five years, through Cladach. It has been a great adventure in learning to sow seeds that fall on all kinds of ground but take root in prepared soil, learning to work with the Wind, keep attuned to the seasons, be willing to engage in cultivation, and give thanks for the harvest.

I thank all this book's readers and reviewers in advance. Gardens and books are for sharing. I hope others will join me as I continue to share in blog form at "On Paths of Prayer and Poetry" (https://prayerandpoetry.com).

Finally, I thank my husband, Larry, who has walked beside me on this path, keeping records, balancing accounts, clearly marking each row, and recording each piece of printed "produce" sent to market. May it all promote health in those who consume it.

CATHERINE LAWTON

Books of Poetry by Catherine Lawton

Available to order wherever books are sold:

REMEMBERING SOFTLY
A Life In Poems

GLIMPSING GLORY
Poems of Living & Dying, Praying & Playing, Belonging & Longing

WHERE ALL THINGS MEET, MIRROR AND MINGLE
(Forthcoming in 2025)

www.ingramcontent.com/pod-product-compliance
Lightning Source LLC
Chambersburg PA
CBHW022109090426
42743CB00008B/775